The English Coast to Coast Walk

What it's really like and how to do it

John Davison

The English Coast to Coast Walk
What it's really like and how to do it

By John Davison

Second edition

Printed by CreateSpace.

Cover picture: Robin Hood's Bay, © 2015, John Davison.

Savour every step. It will be over before you know it.

For Debbie

Contents

Part 1

Chapter 1

The Start

A kind reception, the Irish Sea, wet feet, a lighthouse and a fire, the importance of choosing your own route.

It was late-afternoon when my two-carriage train approached the station at St Bees. Late-afternoon on a bright, sunny day with just a few flimsy, white clouds hanging motionless in the light blue sky.

St Bees station is a small, Victorian affair, built of that hard-looking reddy-brown stone that they often used for civic buildings years ago in the north of England. It's located on a slow, coastal railway line that runs through tiny towns and villages. You know the sort of places. Ones that make you think, "What on earth do people do for a living up here?"

My journey had taken me seven hours but it felt much longer and I couldn't wait to get off the train.

As the little train drew into the station I stood by the carriage door, scanning the platform through the window to discover the exit signs. The train shuddered to a halt and I opened the door and stepped down onto the platform. I was through the ticket barrier and out onto the street in just a few seconds, and then some distance up the street before I realised that I had no idea in which direction I was walking: in my haste to leave the train and get started, I'd neglected to look at my map.

The other passengers who had alighted at St Bees were still fanning out from the station, some met by friends and relatives, some alone. Without exception, they all looked as if they knew where they were going. I didn't want to turn and walk back to the station – that would make me look like what I was: the sole person who didn't know where he was going. I felt a twinge of embarrassment. With my rucksack and walking poles, I looked like a long-distance walker, someone who really *should* know what he's about. So, even though I didn't know where I was going, I kept on a little further then sat down on a low wall to wait until I had the street to myself.

As the hustle and bustle caused by the railway dissipated, I produced my map and took stock. As I suspected, I was walking away from my intended route. I folded the map and started back towards the now deserted station, satisfied that no-one was around to witness my error. I passed the station buildings and walked down towards the coast.

St Bees in May looked a pretty little place. Not up to its peak tourist capacity yet, but in the spring sunshine it looked spruced up and ready for the summer rush. They must see Coast to Coast walkers all the time in St Bees but it seems that familiarity doesn't always breed contempt, because every person I passed stopped to chat with me and, when they found out where I was heading, to wish me luck. I can't think of another place I've been to where someone so obviously transient has been made to feel so genuinely welcome. One elderly man, without any enquiry or prompting from me, told me to take the northern route around Ennerdale Water. "The path on the south side is bloody hard work." I thanked him and told him I'd remember it.

It's traditional at the start of the Coast to Coast Walk to dip your boots into the Irish Sea and to repeat this ritual when you reach the end of the walk at the North Sea. I suppose if you've touched the water at each end of the walk, you can truly say you've walked all the way across the width of the country from sea to sea.

On my way to the beach it occurred to me that I'd need water to prepare my dinner that evening and breakfast the next morning. The beach in front of me was almost empty but the beachfront café was open, so I went in and bought a drink and a snack, just to add on a few extra calories and a bit more fluid. I asked one of the girls behind the counter if she'd mind filling my water bottles and she was happy to oblige. She had never walked the Coast to Coast and, she told me, she had absolutely no ambition to do so.

We chatted until another customer came in to claim her attention and I stepped outside again, into the bright sunshine.

My pack felt much heavier with a couple of litres of water in it and I paused to re-tighten the hip-belt. The beach café was on a slight rise, which gave a good vantage point, and I looked up and down the coast in each direction. The edge of the cloud formation, I noticed, followed the coast almost exactly, so that the sky over the sea was blue and completely clear, while that over the land was dotted with stationary fluffy-white clouds.

I had the promenade to myself as I ambled along it, looking for a bin for my drink can. I reached the stone which marks the start of the walk and took a few photographs. The whole thing felt curiously understated for such a famous walk, I thought. At the very least the situation deserved a brass band (only a small one, of course) and some union jack bunting. Add a cluster of local dignitaries, with the mayor standing in front to shake me by the hand and see me off, and keep the speeches short.

As it was, I didn't even get a bin.

I jumped down from the prom onto the shingle at the top of the beach and looked across it, down to the wet sand and, in the far distance, the sea. I'd intended to carry out the traditional foot-dipping ritual, but the tide was well and truly out and that fact looked as if it would add about a mile to my walk.

Tradition is a good servant but a poor master, and for a moment I considered missing out the shoe-in-the-sea nonsense altogether. But then I told myself not to be churlish. This is the walk of a lifetime and people come from all around the world to hike it. Do it properly, I told myself, or not at all. In any case, the start of this walk had a certain solemnity about it, and it seemed somehow necessary to start the thing properly, so I set off down the beach. The wet sand initially felt firm underfoot, but in fact had enough "give" to slightly sink each foot, so that seawater quickly soaked into my trail shoes. Technically my journey wouldn't start until I had dipped my foot in the sea, so I hadn't even started and already I had wet feet.

Shoe-dipping completed, I strode back up to the promenade with the feeling that my walk was really underway at last.

I quickly reached the end of the prom and started on the footpath leading up the cliffs at the northern end of the bay. The clifftops gave superb views, right back across St Bees and out to sea. In the distance I could see the squat bulk of the Isle of Man, sitting far out on the seaward horizon. The good weather really made the views what they were.

I tend to disbelieve good weather, to regard it with cautious suspicion, and it's a trait which is long-ingrained. A few weeks before I left on this walk, my son and daughter helped my mother tidy out some old things at her house, and in the process they found long-forgotten holiday postcards sent by various members of our family, including me. The holidays were almost always in England, in the summer, and every single postcard contained some reference to the fact that the weather had been bad, combined with optimism that it would soon improve. Maybe it's a characteristic of being English or, at least, of living for a long time in England, that you get used to poor summers and hope the weather will get better. Good weather seems unusual, undeserved, and fleeting, even when we're told to expect it.

On one side, the sea was still and a bright blue, reflecting the sky. On the other side, far across the farm fields, I caught occasional glimpses of the fells[1] of the Lake District, a region I would be crossing very soon.

---

[1] For *fell* and other local terms, see the glossary at page 124.

The top of St Bees Lighthouse appeared over the horizon to my right, and as I walked on along the red dirt path the whole thing gradually came into view.

The first lighthouse on this headland was built in 1718. The short strip of coast between St Bees Head and North Head is the only major sea cliff between Wales and Scotland, so a lighthouse was needed here to protect shipping plying along the coast between the Welsh ports to the south and the Solway Firth to the north. The 1718 light was 9m high and coal-fired. Its design required that loads of coal were carried up to the top of the tower and tipped into a small grate set into the top. Ship-owners complained that their crews couldn't see the light very well, particularly on windy nights when it was often obscured by its own smoke, but the problem was solved, after a fashion, in 1822, when the tower caught fire and burned to the ground. By that time it was, in any case, the last coal-fired lighthouse in England.

The current lighthouse was built in the same year, 1822. It was automated and de-manned in 1987, and it's still in use today.

The clifftops were a beautiful mix of spring colours. A red soil path wound away in front of me; to my right was a field of grass, bright green in the sunshine and dotted with white lambs and ewes; to my left, yellow gorse flowers interspersed with bluebells. Beyond the gorse and the bluebells, the red cliffs dropped down to a foreshore of smashed rock fragments, made black by whatever lichen or algae was growing on them. Beyond the rocky beach, the sea was calm and blue, like something from a children's book. And just to top it all off, a clear blue sky arched over everything.

I could happily have tarried for a while, just to enjoy that view, but I'd only been walking for a few miles and my mind was fixed on forward progress. I thought of something Churchill once said and it kept my feet moving onwards.

"You will never get to the end of the journey if you stop to shy a stone at every dog that barks."

I reached the quarry, where I knew I had to turn right, and started down the track which led away from the coast. As I did so, I mentally bade farewell to the west coast of England. The next time I saw the sea it would signal the end of my journey.

The first few miles of my hike had been easy walking and very enjoyable for that reason, but I found the going much heavier as I went through the marsh at Stanley Pond. The marsh didn't last for long though, and I was soon back on a gravel footpath.

It had been fairly late in the day when I'd started out from St Bees and the evening was starting to draw in, so I started thinking about somewhere to camp for the night. I usually look for somewhere flat enough to put the tent up, reasonably sheltered, and sufficiently secluded so that I don't annoy other people and they don't annoy me, ideally with still enough daylight left for me to prepare and eat my dinner.

I passed through the old mining villages of Moor Row and Cleator without any useful result, and I'd started winding my way up a small hill called Black How before I found a site.

Black How is the western slope of Dent and the latter is usually regarded as the start of the Lake District, so I was right on the boundary as I set up my tent. I pitched it in a small glade, set well back from the track and slightly above it, under some conifer trees. It was an ideal spot for my purpose: quiet, sheltered and private, with a thick layer of pine needles providing a comfortable bed.

Fed and watered, I wriggled down into my sleeping bag, took a nip of whiskey from my hip flask and thought about my walk.

The Coast to Coast Walk was devised by Alfred Wainwright (1907-1991). Wainwright, or A.W. as he liked to be known, was the author of the famous pictorial guides to the Lake District. In 1973 he published what some regard as his crowning glory: a 309km (192 mile) walk across the north of England which takes in the Lake District, the Pennines, the Vale of Mowbray and the North York Moors. The route crosses three national parks and, for the most part, avoids towns.

Wainwright's genius was in constructing a walk which is demanding but which constantly stimulates. He knew the north of England well and he loved it. He applied that knowledge and that love to devise a route which covers the most beautiful parts of England, but which does so in a way which surprises and delights throughout its length. I was to discover that it's difficult to be bored on this walk. Just as you begin to get tired of the ups and downs of the Lake District, you find yourself crossing flat grassland and heading into the Pennines. If the moors start to pall, don't worry: in a few hours you'll find yourself dropping down through farms and villages. I was to pass sites of human activity dating from the prehistoric to the present day and ranging from the pastoral to the industrial. Not for nothing is this one of the most famous walks in the world.

Why do I keep referring to it as the Coast to Coast "Walk" instead of the Coast to Coast "Trail" or the Coast to Coast "Path"? Because there is no cast-iron, set-in-stone route. There is no "trail" as such. There are occasional Coast to Coast signs to be found, but the route as a whole is not waymarked from start to finish as other long distance paths are. A.W. was keen that walkers devise their own long-distance hikes and he encouraged his readers to vary the walk to suit themselves. Indeed, he referred to his route not as "the" Coast to Coast Walk but as "a" Coast to Coast Walk, the idea being that you devise your own route.

In practice, this has led to precisely the opposite happening. The walk is so famous that hikers want to walk *the* Coast to Coast, not just any old coast to coast, and most people stick religiously to the published route. The beauty of the thing, though, is that you can vary the route as you see fit. Add a few miles or take off a few, wander off sight-seeing or put your head down and take the most direct route, and you're still very much in keeping with the spirit of the enterprise. As you slog up, down and across the hard stretches, it would be difficult not to feel A.W.'s deep affection for the countryside through which you're walking. It's not so much his presence which seems to accompany the walker so much as his genuine love for the landscape.

My next few days on the Coast to Coast would be spent walking across the Lake District.

Viewed on a small scale map, the Lake District looks a lot like a wheel, with the mountains forming the spokes radiating out from the centre, and the valleys, often containing lakes, forming the gaps between the spokes. The valleys are mostly steep-sided and flat-floored, and were formed by glaciers in the last ice age which ended 10,000 years ago. The sheer beauty of the area seems to have gone unappreciated until the turn of the nineteenth century when it inspired Wordsworth, Coleridge, Southey and others. The Coast to Coast Walk would take me across the middle of this renowned area of natural beauty, with some of the steepest climbs and descents on the route, and its highest point, Kidsty Pike.

I drifted off to sleep with a sense of pleasant anticipation which is, of course, the best kind of anticipation.

I woke early the next morning. I'd slept well, but the pine needles had proved lumpier than I'd expected: uncomfortable enough to annoy me, but not so much as to make me get up and do something about it, so I didn't exactly spring from my woodland bed.

It was some time before I got myself organised and started walking again. I realised that I'd got out of practice at doing all the things that had to be done first thing in the morning, but I knew I'd speed up as the walk went on.

I reached the top of Dent and paused to admire the views. Behind me the land stretched away to the coast, overhung by thin, high clouds against a blue sky. Ahead I could see the dark masses of the Lake District peaks, with an additional, lower layer of cloud at about the same height as me. I strained my eyes and tried to make out my route into the Lakes.

Chapter 2

The Lake District

The remotest hostel in England, the founder of the London Marathon, self-acting inclines, plumbago, the sad story of Gordon Hallworth, and a model community.

I made my way down from Dent and walked across Raven Crag. The path dropped steeply to Nannycatch Beck, so steeply that I had to take care not to slip and turn a knee or an ankle.

Nannycatch Beck is a stream that runs in a deep ravine and when I got to the bottom of it, the valley floor felt like a little world all of its own, quiet and secluded with just the beck burbling along.

There was a distinct chill in Nannycatch, the steep, green sides of the valley keeping me in their shade. Stands of bluebells made distant grey patches on the valley sides, getting bluer as I approached them. A lone farmhouse higher up on the east side looked down on me. I wondered if anyone there had seen me pass. If they had, would they care? I suspected not.

Soon the land opened out and I was at Low Cock How, close to Kinniside Stone Circle. I didn't dally at Kinniside: it's a nice spot, but the stone circle is a modern recreation rather than a prehistoric original, and I still had work to do. I pressed on and I was soon at Ennerdale Bridge.

Ennerdale Bridge is a small village which nevertheless generates sufficient custom to support two pubs. The Fox and

Hounds looked a good bet, so I pulled over to give them some custom. I was an hour early, however, so I spent a relaxing hour sitting by the stream, in the dappled sunshine of the pub's garden.

A couple of pints later, I was back on the trail again, this time heading for my first lake on this walk: Ennerdale Water.

I reached the north-west corner of the lake and paused by the weir to take in the view. Ennerdale Water was calm and flat and grey. On the opposite side and 250m above me, the mound of Bowness Knott should have looked significant, but it was dwarfed by the unlikely named Great Borne and Starling Dodd behind it, both well over 600m in height. I knew I would pass many lakes on this walk, but Ennerdale Water was the first of them and felt special for that reason. I'm not the only person who rates the place: Bill Clinton proposed to Hillary here in 1973.

I had two route options from this point: I could follow the path around the south shore of Ennerdale Water or take the track around the north side of the lake. I knew a little of the north side from previous walking trips and I remembered the advice of the man in St Bees, "The path on the south side is bloody hard work," so I set off up the north side of the water.

I was walking along a gravel track and, from each side, broadleaved trees arched over my head, splendid with their new, bright-green spring leaves. Sunbeams filtered through wherever they found a gap in the forest canopy, patching the track with sunny spots.

I reached Ennerdale Youth Hostel at mid-afternoon and found that I had a two hour wait before reception opened. I'd had a short day yesterday and I hadn't walked a full day today, but that was all part of my cunning plan. I've learned from experience that it suits me best if I gradually work my way in to a long walk, rather than starting full-bore on the first day. Two progressively harder days, leading up to a full day's walking on day three should, I felt, be just the ticket.

Unfortunately, my plan left me with two hours to kill. I hate the phrase "killing time". Time rushes by far too quickly without us making an extra effort to kill it, but I made myself a coffee and carried it through to the hostel's lounge. Then I lounged. It was the price, I told myself, of a sensible and graduated start to my walk.

Eventually the hostel came to life and I secured a room of six beds, all to myself. There were five other guests: an elderly British couple and three Australian women. Like me, the Aussies were backpacking the Coast to Coast walk, but I was taken aback by the loads they were carrying. In addition to an awful lot of hiking gear, one of them had ten days' worth of food on her back, with the blistered feet that such a heavy load will cause. It was only the second day of their trek and while there's never a good time for it, I couldn't help feeling that Day Two was a bit early to have your feet rubbed raw. They were in good spirits, though, and cheerful company at dinner.

If I needed a reminder of how quickly the weather can change in these parts, I got it the next morning. The blue sky, the sunshine and the sun-dappled path were all gone, replaced by low, black, swirling clouds, with more cloud higher up, visible through the gaps. The lower cloud must have been at about 500m, completely blanking out the hilltops around me and feeling like a very low ceiling over the valley of Ennerdale. As I stepped out into the thickening drizzle, I knew I'd need to take extra care over navigation, particularly when I got up into the cloud.

I pulled on my waterproofs and started walking up the valley towards Black Sail Hut, watched with interest by the Galloway cattle, standing mute between the trees alongside the track.

Black Sail is the remotest of all the premises managed by the Youth Hostel Association. Once a shepherd's hut, it became a youth hostel in 1933, famed for its isolation and its somewhat Spartan living conditions. Its very existence had been at risk a few years before my visit because, as part of the re-wilding of the valley, the *Wilding Ennerdale* project had planned to remove the jeep track that supplies the hostel. Thankfully the jeep track has been spared and with it the hostel, the latter being renovated to make it more sustainable.

Once there, in return for a trifling donation, I managed to get some tea and a piece of cake from one of the staff, and I took time to admire the renovation of the hostel. They seemed to have kept the spirit of the place, but I was disappointed to find that the plaque in memory of Chris Brasher was no longer on the wall.

Chris Brasher was a remarkable man. In 1954 he acted as a pacemaker for Roger Bannister when Bannister ran the first sub-four minute mile. Two years later Brasher won a gold medal in the Melbourne Olympics. He was one of the first people to take part in the sport of orienteering in Britain and one of the founders of the London Marathon. The plaque in his memory, which used to be on the wall in Black Sail Hut, read:

Chris Brasher CBE
1928 - 2003

Olympic athlete, mountaineer, journalist, businessman and philanthropist

"Ah, but a man's reach should exceed his grasp, or what's a heaven for?" Robert Browning

A lifetime of love and support for outdoor sport and for the world's wild places. A benefactor to the YHA and outdoor activity in the Lakes. Spent his last night hostelling with friends, at Black Sail on 29 June 2002 – "a disgraceful episode at which we devoured 14 different curries and consumed nine bottles of good Australian wine!"

This plaque erected by his friends in OBOE – 'On the Back Of an Envelope' – the way Chris believed any worthwhile expedition can be planned.

The plaque was such an integral part of the history of the

place that I asked the lady from the Youth Hostel Association where it was and whether it would be put back up.

She told me that the plaque was unlikely to be put back on the wall. It was not, she went on, the image desired by the current management of the Youth Hostel Association. She didn't seem too enamoured by the current management of the Youth Hostel Association and I got the impression that this wasn't the first time she'd been asked about the plaque. "A benefactor of the YHA" quite possibly, but no longer one they wish to acknowledge. It was with a little sadness that I left Black Sail Hut and pressed on up Ennerdale.

I turned left up Loft Beck and started walking north-east, up the steep, step-sized slabs of rock, while next to me the rainwater in the beck splashed and tumbled its way to the River Liza down below in Ennerdale. The clouds lifted as I climbed, as if they wanted to keep the same distance away from me, but the sky stayed a stubborn, constant grey.

I reached the top of my climb and the ground levelled out, enabling me to get my breath back. I could see Buttermere and Crummock Water to the north, scenic high points even in this lovely setting. I skirted the flank of Grey Knotts and gained the old tramway which leads down to Honister Slate Mine.

Completed in 1891, the tramway was a self-acting incline which linked Dubbs Quarry, higher up the fell, with the slate mine down below at Honister. Slate was mined at Dubbs Quarry and loaded onto trucks which ran on rails. A four-horse team pulled each train of trucks to the high point on the fell and it was here that the self-acting system took over. Gravity caused the trucks to descend the incline to Honister and the downward motion of the heavy trucks was used to pull the empties back up the hill to the waiting horse teams, which would pull them back to Dubbs Quarry to be reloaded. The "incline" proved a very efficient way of moving slate and several were constructed in the neighbouring hills to carry slate to Honister. Reportedly, one was still in use in the 1960s.

I was looking forward to Honister because the slate mine there has a tea shop. Simple pleasures count for a lot when I'm walking and I was eagerly hoping to get a coffee simply by asking for it and placing money on the counter, with no need to assemble my stove or search out my mug, water, spoon and so on.

Honister has the last working slate mine in England. Mining started here in 1728 but was probably going on in some form since Roman times, and Honister slate was sent near and far, used on famous buildings and on humble shops and homes. Buckingham Palace and Scotland Yard are both roofed with Honister slate. Demand dwindled when builders started using roofing tiles and schools stopped using slates, and nowadays the mine is mainly a tourist attraction.

I left without buying any slate souvenirs – I had 260km still to walk and my legs told me I had quite enough to carry as it was.

I passed through the hamlet of Seatoller, the day's destination for the Australian girls I'd met at High Gillerthwaite, last night's hostel. It was 11am and if that distance constituted a full day's walking for them, I knew I wouldn't see them again on this trip.

A small lane leads away from Seatoller to the even smaller hamlet of Seathwaite, just 2km away. In 1555 an unusually solid form of graphite was discovered at Seathwaite, to this day the only deposit of graphite ever found in this solid form[2]. It was mined for many years and Seathwaite graphite eventually became the principal ingredient for the Keswick pencil-making industry. Over the centuries many types mineral have been mined in Cumbria, but graphite was the most valuable of them. Theft and smuggling were rife, and for many years armed guards protected the mine around the clock. After nearly three and a half centuries of mining, extraction finally ceased in 1891.

Seathwaite has one other peculiarity: it's the wettest inhabited place in England, averaging 140 inches of rain a year. Nearly twelve feet of rain each and every year! I checked what

---

[2] Graphite is also known as *black lead, wad* and *plumbago.*

the clouds were doing and hurried on, giving Seathwaite a wide berth.

I got off of the road as soon as I could and followed the path downhill towards the village of Rosthwaite. Someone had gone to great lengths to fix chains to the rocks along the side of the River Derwent to act as handrails, but I couldn't see why. The rocks were perfectly walkable as they were and if the river flooded the chains would be under water and useless. I strolled along next to them, wondering if they had some old, long-forgotten purpose which I couldn't fathom.

As I was walking by the Derwent, the sun came out. No warning, no preamble. One moment it was cloudy and murky, the next the sun was straight out, in a no-nonsense, Northern sort of way. By the time I reached Rosthwaite it had all the makings of a nice day.

Rosthwaite is in Borrowdale, a valley which used to be known for its copper and graphite mining, and its iron smelting and charcoal burning. Today, all that has long gone and the dale looks the very epitome of calm, rural, English charm.

I thought I'd save some time by asking a local for directions to the nearest pub, but the man I chose seemed to be, if not the village idiot, at least a strong contender for the position. He solemnly assured me there was no pub or hotel in Rosthwaite. He spoke with forked tongue, though, and I knew that with a high degree of certainty because I'd done my research before I left home. I was tempted to tell him that the tradition of the village idiot is one we could happily leave behind us in the 21st century, but of course I didn't. Instead, I did the English thing and politely thanked him for his help.

I found a pub just a few minutes later and sat outside in the sunshine with my food. I was hungry and I gave free rein to my appetite, then sat back on my seat for just one more drink and applied some sun cream to my neck and face. Rosthwaite had served me pretty well, I reflected. William Wordsworth was less fortunate when he stayed here and noted sniffily that he "had to share a bed with a Scotch pedlar". The feelings of the Scotch pedlar are not recorded.

Stonethwaite Beck was a lovely walk in the shade of the trees, with their new foliage, but there weren't many trees and I was soon out in the full sun as the path steepened along Greenup Gill.

Ahead of me, by the side of the path, I could see a stone with a plaque fixed to it.

I can never walk past a notice or a sign without stopping to study it, so I paused to read this one. It was more interesting than most. It reads:

THIS TABLET WAS AFFIXED BY
DOUGLAS AND MICHAEL BOYLE
IN ENDURING MEMORY
OF THEIR FRIEND AND COMPANION
GORDON HALLWORTH
WHO DIED IN PEACE
UNDER THE SHELTER OF THIS ROCK
IN THE EARLY HOURS OF SUNDAY
8TH JANUARY 1939

As a further memorial, a footbridge was erected over nearby Greenup Gill and a tablet on it adds that Gordon was "a devoted member of Manchester University Mountaineering Club". He was just 21 years old when he died "notwithstanding the self-sacrificing assistance of his two companions and the strenuous efforts of a relief party".

The plaques make it sound as if Gordon died in some benighted outpost of empire, but in fact he was here in England, a mere two miles along an easy path from the hamlet of Stonethwaite. How could this have happened?

The incident made headlines all over the country, but perhaps those on the front page of the Nottingham Evening Post summed up the sad story most succinctly:

TRAGIC STORY OF THE CUMBERLAND FELLS

STUDENTS FIGHT TO SAVE COLLEAGUE'S LIFE

BEATEN BY WASHED AWAY BRIDGE

HELD UP FOR HOURS: UNABLE TO CROSS STREAM

It's difficult to decipher the social sensitivities of a 1930s inquest and get at the facts of the matter, but most of the details are clear and undisputed.

On Saturday 7th January 1939, three Manchester University students, brothers Douglas and Michael Boyle, and their friend Gordon Hallworth, were out walking on the fells. On their way back, they arrived at the junction of two streams, Greenup Gill and Langstrath Beck. Both streams were in spate and the trio found that they were unable to cross because the bridge they were expecting to use had been washed away. They decided to walk back up Greenup Gill to look for a suitable place to cross it.

Gordon began to show signs of distress and Michael had to support him as they walked. Gordon's distress evidently worsened because Douglas had to lend a hand too, and eventually the Boyles had to carry Gordon. At one point they stopped to rest but that made them cold and they had to huddle together for warmth.

Michael managed to get across Greenup Gill with the aid of a pole, but even with that he found it difficult to cross. Next, the brothers tried to get Gordon across, but he fell into the stream. Michael got him to the bank and together they began to descend Greenup Gill.

Gordon suggested many times that the Boyles should leave him because he was holding them back, but they refused and tried to keep his spirits up by talking about the dinner they would have later that evening.

Michael found it hard work assisting Gordon down the hill and began to fall. Soon all three of them kept falling over.

Gordon was unable to go any further, so the Boyles left

him in the shelter of a boulder and went to get help.

Michael was the next to collapse and Douglas was forced to go on alone, arriving in Rosthwaite at 1.30am on Sunday 8th.

A rescue party was organised and a Doctor Alec Martin went out with them. Martin found Gordon Hallworth in the shelter of the large stone where the Boyles had left him. He was dead.

Emotions must still have been tender when the inquest was held because, in the custom of the time, it commenced (and concluded) the very next day. It was held in Rosthwaite and chaired by Her Majesty's Coroner, Col D. Mason.

The inquest heard that there were a lot of other people out walking on the fells that day and that the walk had been well within Hallworth's capabilities, notwithstanding the foul weather. He had accustomed himself to being on the hills in bad weather and he'd been out in much worse, and subjected himself to greater strain, witnesses said. Gordon's father told the inquest that his son, while not robust, was "wiry" and always surprised him by how much he could do.

In answer to the Coroner, Douglas Boyle pointed out that the three did not consider their walk "an undertaking". It was the shortest walk they could do, he said, and they would have been back by teatime had the bridge over Greenup Gill been intact.

The inquest returned a verdict of "Death from exhaustion due to exposure to the cold".

The newspapers don't give details of the route taken by the Manchester students or of their day's walking, but we can make some deductions.

We know that they tried to use the bridge where Greenup Gill meets Langstrath Beck and, when they found the bridge was out, they walked back up Greenup to find a place to cross. Their movements, and the fact that Langstrath Beck is bigger than Greenup Gill and would have been even more formidable to cross, suggests that they were at the base of Bleak Howe, trying to cross Greenup Gill from south-west to north-east. The location of the current bridge, put up in memory of Gordon

Hallworth, would seem to support this.

The three made their way back up Greenup Gill and were able to cross it, although Gordon went into the stream in the process. Gordon probably got soaked when he fell in. Given that he was already showing signs of distress to the extent that he couldn't walk without help, that drenching must have been a big psychological blow as well as putting him at risk of hypothermia.

Next, Hallworth and the Boyles made their way north-west, along the path to Rosthwaite. The boulder where Gordon died is on this path and so marks that point on their route.

Although we don't know how far they walked during the day, on the ground these last few miles do not look challenging.

On the other hand, the weather seems to have presented a significant test in its own right.

Inclement weather is always to be expected in January, particularly in the fells of the Lake District, but January 1939 was exceptional for its bad weather. The temperature across the country was appreciably below average for the time of year, but especially so in the north (although the highest temperatures of the month were recorded on the 7th and the 8th, the dates the Boyles and Hallworth were out on the hills). The Meteorological Office records show January 1939 as "A notably wet month". Some parts of the UK received *three times* their usual rainfall and the Met Office estimated it to be the wettest January since 1764, 165 years earlier.

So: colder than average, torrential rain and serious flooding. That gives an idea of why the footbridge across Greenup Gill had been washed away and why the stream was so difficult to ford. It also gives an indication of how dangerous the situation would have been for Gordon Hallworth after he was immersed in Greenup Gill. And let's not forget that Gordon was showing signs of distress even before he went into the stream.

Were the three students experienced enough to be out walking at that time of year in bad weather? Could they have reasonably anticipated such bad weather? Were they properly equipped and fit enough? Or had they taken on too great a challenge?

Interestingly, the Coroner in this case noted that, "This was precisely the same kind of thing which had happened in that valley four or five years ago … on a similar kind of day". He thought that the Boyles and Hallworth "might have a greater respect for the difficulties that arose in that district", and he made a point of stating that he was not suggesting they were inexperienced.

Was Colonel Mason implying that the three students should have known better? I'll leave that to you to decide.

I hadn't seen another soul since Rosthwaite, and the empty valley and the story of Gordon Hallworth made me feel very lonely as I kept on up Greenup Edge and over Lining Crag. A mile of bog-hopping followed and then I was heading downhill once again, following Far Easedale Gill down Easedale to Grasmere.

Easedale is a beautiful valley. Even though I was starting to feel the effects of the day's exertions, I thoroughly enjoyed picking my way downhill, over the stream and back again, an experience made even more enjoyable when I entered the fields and the woods below Helm Crag. Helm Crag is also known as The Lion and the Lamb, because of its outline. Less impressively, it's also known as The Old Lady at the Piano because of the way it looks from another direction. The path comes out in Grasmere, which Wordsworth thought, "The loveliest spot that man hath ever found." Argue with that if you can. I couldn't.

I spent a comfortable night in Grasmere and I stepped back onto the trail the next morning beneath low, fast-moving clouds. The clouds stuck to the valleys, staying well below the surrounding hilltops, but I could see patches of blue beyond them, higher up. The fields in the valley bottom and the trees lining the lower slopes of the valley sides seemed to contain just about every possible shade of green.

I set a steady pace uphill on a farm track, moving into the

early-morning mist which seemed to rise with me as I gained height. It was a steep pull up Little Tongue Gill, past the new hydro-electric plant, and even steeper up to Grisedale Tarn. By now I was much higher up and cooled by a strong breeze as I walked. The valley was covered with that sparse, wiry sort of grass that you find on British hills, interspersed with a few patches of rock debris, and the morning mist had risen and metamorphosed into solid grey cloud overhead.

I'd intended to stop for a cup of tea at Grisedale Tarn but when I got there I discovered it wasn't a good resting place. The tarn sits in the pass which runs between two hills, Dollywaggon Pike and Fairfield. There was plenty of water in the tarn and it certainly wouldn't have missed a cupful to make my tea, but the wind was whistling through the pass, making it an inhospitable location. I decided to drop down to calmer slopes before I started fiddling with my stove.

I started my descent into Grisedale, towards what was clearly better weather further down the valley, and by the time I got to Ruthwaite Lodge I had to stop and fish out my sun hat.

Ruthwaite Lodge was locked up but it looked in good condition. The lodge was an old hunting stop, almost derelict by the 1950s when it was taken over and restored by Sheffield University Mountaineering Club to create a climbers' hut. The club folded in 2001 and there's no sign of who currently owns the lodge. A plaque on the outside wall remembers two Outward Bound tutors who fell to their deaths from 12,000 feet Mount Cook in New Zealand, in 1988.

Like a lot of the Lake District, this area was mined extensively in times past. Lead was mined in Ruthwaite Cove, just a little way up the hill to the west of the lodge, and several underground mines and surface workings were operated, beginning in the 1500s, with further leases taken out in 1784 and 1862. Mining eventually became uneconomic and the last activity at Ruthwaite was in 1880.

I stopped to chat with the only other people I'd seen since breakfast: a retired couple from Philadelphia. After only a few minutes, I had another place to add to my bucket list.

I carried on and I was soon through the intake wall[3], strolling down a gravel track through sheep pastures towards the deep-green trees of Patterdale. The valley looked lovely, with a proportion and a beauty which stood out, even in this part of the country which is known for its scenic hills and dales. I remembered that Patterdale was Wainwright's favourite valley and I could see why.

I ate lunch in the White Lion in Patterdale and looked enviously at the sent-ahead-by-van suitcases of other Coast to Coast walkers, piled in one corner of the bar. Walking with baggage transfer and staying at pubs? I made a mental note to try it one day, maybe when I'm old and infirm.

I paid up and wandered back out of the pub. There was a bench nearby so I invested a few minutes and checked my feet and my shoes. Satisfied that all was well, I set off north-east from Patterdale.

The walk across the narrow floodplain of Goldrill Beck was lovely but short - the valley bottom is not wide in this part of Patterdale - and then I turned through ninety degrees and started diagonally up the steep valley side towards Boredale Hause.

A small rectangle of stones, roughly three metres by seven, at the top of Boredale Hause looks like an old animal pen or the remains of a shepherd's hut. In fact this is *Chapel in the Hause* and the dilapidated stone walls are all that remains of an early medieval church built high-up, here on the fell, to serve the residents of Patterdale on one side of the hill and Martindale on the other. It can't have looked very different in November 1805 when William and Dorothy Wordsworth climbed the fell here. Dorothy recorded it as looking more like "a common sheepfold" than a church. I left, wondering about the devotion of people who would make such a fiercely steep ascent just to go to a church service, not to mention the social pressures which

---

[3] The *intake wall* is the last wall that separates cultivated farmland from the open hill. It refers to the land below it, which has been "taken in" from the hill.

compelled them to do so.

There were a few day-walkers out on the fell, including family groups and they, as much as the views out across Ullswater, gave the place a feeling of being cherished and special. It was good to see quite small children so obviously enjoying the outdoors.

I'd left them all behind though, by the time I reached Angle Tarn, and I was on my own in the hills once again. I rounded The Knott and then had to take a moment to work out which hill was which, so as to be sure I was going the right way.

To my right was the peak of High Street, so called because of the old Roman road which runs along its summit. In those days the valleys were full of woodland and marsh, so I guess a road across the fells offered quicker transport and enhanced personal safety.

Just before High Street was Racecourse Hill, a flattish area where shepherds from the surrounding fells used to meet to race, and eat and drink. The last gathering was in 1830, but the name survives.

Straight ahead of me, the path led up to a pyramidal peak named Kidsty Pike. At 780m above sea level, Kidsty Pike would be the highest point on my walk. Wordsworth described it as "The loneliest place of all these hills" and I was starting to see what he meant.

Between High Street and Kidsty Pike, at about one o'clock from where I was standing, was Riggindale, a deep glacial valley and home of England's last golden eagle. Conservation charities have decided not to reintroduce any prospective mates for him. Instead, bizarrely, the eagle will simply be left to die, rendering the species extinct in England. I was almost glad I wasn't able to see him – it would have been an emotional moment to witness something like that in the knowledge that it was on its way to extinction.

I crested Kidsty Pike at about teatime and stopped to take in the views, which were magnificent in every direction. Below me lay Haweswater, flat and blue, looking for all the world as if it had been there for centuries. There were patches of woodland around the edges of the lake, and the fresh-looking green of the trees made a pleasing contrast against the paler, grassy fells. Beyond Haweswater, on the far, far horizon, I could just make out the Pennines, the next mountainous obstacle on my route, just a thin, grey line away in the distance. I ate some chocolate, thinking as I did so that it was the view that was high-calorie here.

When I'd had enough of the view, I started picking my way carefully down the steep east side of Kidsty Pike towards Haweswater, in what used to be the valley of Mardale.

The original, natural lake in this valley was quite small. Then, in the 1930s, Haweswater Beck was dammed to create the reservoir which would help meet the growing demand for water from the city of Manchester.

The project was a controversial one right from the start, not least because it involved the complete demolition of two villages and the forced relocation of their inhabitants. Despite all that, in 1919, Parliament passed the Act which allowed Manchester Corporation to build the dam. Preparatory work started in the 1920s and in 1930 the Lord Mayor of Manchester detonated the first explosion to start work on the dam proper.

The dam was designed so that, as the retained water presses against it, the dam is supported and strengthened by hollow buttresses which enable it to take the pressure. Haweswater was the first "hollow buttress" dam in the world and it was, and remains, the highest dam in Britain. In order to make it, the residents of two villages, Mardale Green and Measand, were resettled elsewhere and their villages were demolished. Stone from the church in Mardale Green was recycled to build the dam and the bodies of those buried in the churchyard were exhumed and reinterred in Shap, 8km away. During World War 2 many of the dam builders were "called up" into the armed services, but nevertheless the dam was completed in 1940. It took two years to fill and raised the level of the lake by 30m. Ever since its completion, the water it supplies travels over 100 miles south to Manchester by gravity alone – there are no pumps.

I was getting tired and dehydrated, and I stumbled like a drunk down the steep hill to the lake, pausing to eat a snack and drink some water in an effort to put some vitality into my legs. I could spare the water, I felt. There were nineteen thousand million gallons of the stuff right in front of me[4].

I reached the lakeside near Speaking Crag. The lake and the few trees nearby were completely still as I fished out my map. I was very aware that I was on a deadline here: I had to camp within a reasonable distance of the village of Shap because, sitting in the post office at Shap, was my first food parcel and tomorrow was a Saturday. That meant I had to collect my parcel by 1230 or wait until the post office opened after the weekend, at 9 o'clock on Monday morning. I had no doubt that the attractions of Shap were many and varied, but I didn't want to be kicking my heels in the place for a full weekend.

I'd hoped there might be a vehicle track along the shore of the reservoir but there was only a thin, winding footpath. I was tired and I'd planned to camp as soon as I reached the water, but I realised that I wouldn't make good time along the footpath next morning, so there was no alternative but to keep going and to camp nearer the dam. Eventually, I decided I'd got myself close enough to the dam and I managed to find a flat area just off the path. It was secluded from prying eyes and big enough to accommodate my little tent, and I pitched camp. The evening was quiet and still, with just enough breeze to keep the grass and the tent dry, but not enough to chill me. I realised that I hadn't seen another soul since before Angle Tarn. I made dinner and watched the sun set behind the hills I'd just crossed. I was quickly in shadow and then it was dark. Time for bed.

I woke at 5.30am, to a golden glow behind a few high, grey clouds. Dawn. There was still no-one about. It was an idyllic spot and I actually enjoyed my morning routine in the

---

[4] I haven't invented that figure: it is the actual capacity of Haweswater Reservoir.

early sunshine. I shouldered my pack and set off across the grass, back to the reservoir path again.

The first thing I saw as I regained the path was a large sign stating *No Camping.* I'd never have seen it the previous evening unless I'd walked further along the footpath, so I didn't feel I'd done anything wrong. But it did occur to me that if anyone had come up the path from the dam, they would have seen a large no camping sign and my tent almost directly underneath it.

I wondered whether the reservoir authorities were serious about their no camping rule. As Britain has become more litigious, it seems to me that many signs banning activities are put up not so much to ban the activity as to frustrate lawsuits if anything goes wrong. I recalled a holiday in a little town on the south coast. Signs all along the seafront banned skateboarding and roller-skating, with dire threats of prosecution and fines. But in the two weeks I spent there, there was so much skateboarding and roller-skating that you could have been forgiven for thinking the seafront was some sort of skate-park. I never saw any enforcement action, nor anyone who looked as if they might be council workers. My theory is that those signs were put up not to ban skateboarding but to prevent skateboarders from suing the council if they got hurt. If anyone suffered an accident and tried to plead that the council should have made the place safer, the council could simply say, "You shouldn't have been skateboarding. We put up signs."

The problem with this approach is that we can't differentiate between activities which are unlawful, I mean *really* unlawful, and those which no-one cares about provided we pursue them at our own risk. I had no idea whether United Utilities, the current operators of the reservoir, genuinely did not want me to camp there, or whether they just wanted to avoid liability if anything went wrong when I did camp there. In any event, the deed was done and I still had to get to Shap, so I moved on.

I enjoyed the last of the walk along the reservoir. I was still 7km from my food parcel, but I knew I could walk that quite easily in the time available to me.

I reached the dam at the end of the reservoir and dropped downhill to the village of Burnbanks.

Burnbanks consists of a few small bungalows with an air of prefabrication about them, arranged around a village green with a red telephone box.

When the dam was built, this rural, isolated area was unable to supply the workforce required and hundreds of unemployed workers were recruited from across the north of England. Because of the remoteness of the place, they lodged in local farmhouses at first. But then, instead of the usual labourers' encampment which was the norm for this sort of undertaking, Manchester Corporation came good: the city built a model village especially for the dam builders and their families.

66 dwellings were put up, cast-iron, prefabricated bungalows with all the mod cons of the 1930s. With electricity, hot and cold running water, and modern kitchens and bathrooms, they must have been the envy of many locals. The Corporation also provided a mission, a canteen, a dispensary, a recreation hall, a shop, and tennis courts and allotments. They paid for a policeman, a nurse and a shopkeeper, and financed the expansion of the local school at Bampton, 2.5km away. 315 people lived in Burnbanks in the 1930s, but as the work finished, the population inevitably dwindled. Now, the village is only a fraction of what it was.

I passed through a bluebell wood which made me briefly homesick for my local woods in Essex, and reached Naddle Bridge, the old 18th century road bridge over Haweswater Beck.

I crossed Haweswater Beck and found my first "trail magic": a box of snacks and drinks with an honesty box for walkers to leave money in payment for whatever they take. It was a simple thing but it added to the general good feeling which was pervading the morning.

I was crossing farmland now, deep green pastures under a bright, blue sky, with just a few high, wispy cirrus clouds. I dropped downhill to Shap Abbey, passing another honesty box, but this one was full of litter and rain water.

Shap Abbey or, to give it its proper name, the Abbey Church of St Mary Magdalene, is now only a ruined tower and a few farm buildings, but it must have been an impressive sight when the Premonstratensian order built it in 1199.

The Premonstratensian monks at Shap escaped the first phase of the Dissolution of the Monasteries in 1536, but in 1540 the abbey was closed down and its assets were seized by the Crown[5]. Some parts of the abbey were taken over as farm buildings and remain so to this day, while others were demolished and the stone recycled into local farms and houses.

A short distance further on and I was walking through those houses as I entered Shap. Shap is a linear village, stretched along the main A6 road, a characteristic which made it easy to find the post office part way along. The Post Master was helpful and I was soon back out, clutching my parcel and trying not to feel like a prisoner of war who has just received his first Red Cross package.

I found a bench a little further up the main street and sat down in the sunshine to open my parcel. There was a cold wind blowing but I wasn't deterred. I wanted to discard the parcel wrapping and any unnecessary packaging inside it before I put the food away and moved on. It's slightly bizarre, and it's no exaggeration to say it, but I felt like a small kid at Christmas. Sweets! I'd forgotten that I'd packed those. Chocolate! Better make a start on that right now.

I stuck the detritus in a nearby bin and moved off with more to carry, but with that warm feeling that some of us get from self-sufficiency and independence. Combined with the occasional pub meal, I now had enough food to get me to Richmond or beyond, a hundred kilometres away. So it was with a lightness of foot and a general feeling of goodwill to all humankind that I walked through the backstreets of Shap and

---

[5] The *Dissolution of the Monasteries* was a legal process instituted by King Henry VIII between 1536 and 1541 by which Catholic monasteries, priories, etc, were disbanded, their inhabitants pensioned off and their assets appropriated by the Crown.

across the fields to the M6 motorway.

The M6 was another threshold. It's generally regarded, particularly on the Coast to Coast Walk, as the dividing line between the Lake District and the Pennines. For that reason, crossing the little footbridge felt hugely symbolic, despite the mind-numbing noise generated by the six lanes of traffic beneath me.

I lingered for a moment and looked back. I could just make out the angular peak of Kidsty Pike behind me on the far horizon.

I turned and completed my crossing of the motorway.

Chapter 3

The Pennines

Ancient stone circles, a Royalist army marching to battle, a bed in a church, coffin stones and corpse roads, bell pits and hushing.

A whole new world lay ahead of me.

While I'd spent the occasional walking weekend in the Lakes and knew a little of that area as a result, I'd never experienced the Pennines before. I knew that most of the ascent and descent on my walk was to be found in the Lake District, so I hoped the Pennines might be kind to me.

The Pennines are a range of limestone hills running down the length of northern England and are often referred to as "the backbone of England". Their climate is not very dissimilar to that in the rest of the UK, but I expected them to be wetter and windier because hills generally are. And I seemed to remember reading somewhere that part of the Pennine chain has a sub-Arctic climate.

Whatever the ins and outs of it, the weather was glorious as I strode across the hill and past the quarry, on the way to Oddendale. Already I could see the land changing, becoming greener and less mountainous.

The hills ahead of me looked desolate and empty of people, but it wasn't always so. On my right was Oddendale Stone Circle, a double-ringed Neolithic circle of wooden posts which were removed and replaced with granite blocks in the early Bronze Age[6]. Excavations here discovered cremated bone, pottery and token grave goods, indicating that this was a site of some importance for many hundreds of years. To my left were Seal Howe Cairns, two Bronze Age burial sites. When they were excavated in 1877, they contained an unburnt male and, in a secondary burial, the cremated remains of a woman and a child in an urn. A few ox bones were also found. A little further on, my route would cross an old Roman road. Although it might not be obvious, human activity in this area has been extensive and occurred over a very long period.

I crossed my first limestone pavement, something I'd learned about many years ago in school but never seen for real until now. I stopped and bent down to examine the clints and grikes.

A short distance off the path here is Black Dub Monument, a stone obelisk next to the pool of water from which Lyvennet Beck flows away northwards. The inscription on the obelisk reads:

HERE AT BLACK DUB
THE SOURCE OF THE LIVENNET
KING CHARLES II
REGALED HIS ARMY
AND DRANK OF THE WATER
ON HIS MARCH FROM SCOTLAND
AUGUST 8 1651

By August 1651, Parliament had to all intents and purposes won the English Civil War. King Charles I had been tried, executed in Whitehall, and England was a republic. His son was proclaimed King Charles II by the Scots and he marched south into England with an army, intending to retake

---

[6] In the UK, the *Neolithic* (or New Stone Age) ran from roughly 4000BCE to 2500BCE, the *Bronze Age* from 2500BCE to 700BCE, and the *Iron Age* from 700BCE to 500BCE.

the English throne and paused here at Black Dub on the way.

But it was not to be: in September, Charles and his Scottish allies were routed at Worcester by Oliver Cromwell and the Parliamentary army. From a force of 16,000 Royalist soldiers, 3,000 were killed and 10,000 captured. Of those, 8,000 (mostly Scots) were forcibly deported to work on the plantations in New England and the West Indies. Charles fled into exile in Europe and the Civil war was over.

The sun was blazing down now, and I dug my sun hat out of my pack and smeared some sun cream on my neck. It was getting near to lunchtime and I was close to one of those pub meal opportunities that reduce the weight of food I have to carry, so I decided to drop down into Orton and see what was available.

I trekked downhill towards the village, marvelling at the vibrancy of colour in the blue sky and the green fields in the sunshine. I knew this could be a harsh environment if the weather changed, but I had no idea it could be so beautiful. I was to discover that the north of England is by no means all cobbles, soot and whippets.

I followed a stream through the fields, then passed a few large, well-maintained houses with expensive cars on their drives, and there was The George Hotel right in front of me. It was far too lovely a day to sit inside, so I found a table outside in the beer garden, tarted myself up a bit and ordered lunch.

The food at The George was superb although, to be fair, by Day 5 of a long walk, anything I can cram into my mouth counts as superb food and that goes double if ketchup is available. One large meal and a couple of pints later, and I was right as rain. I strode out of Orton in the highest of spirits.

Just up the road I passed Gamelands Stone Circle. Maybe it was because I'd already passed Oddendale and Seal Howe or, more likely, because I was born and grew up between Avebury and Stonehenge, but I found Oddendale Circle distinctly underwhelming. It consists of 43 boulders, none of them more than a metre high, in an embanked "circle" about 42m by 35m.

In fairness, the stones were pulled over and some of them were blasted into bits to make a wall when the field was ploughed in the 1860s, so they have had a hard time of it.

When I started passing Great Ewe Fell, I knew I was near to Bents Farm, my intended destination for the day. Bents Farm was shown on my map as a bunkhouse and I rather fancied a conventional bed for the night.

As I got close to Bents Farm, I didn't like the look of it. The field I was standing in had been torn up into huge ruts by some sort of massive agricultural machinery. The result scarred the landscape and made walking difficult, and the farm, from what I could see of it across the valley, looked more dilapidated than welcoming. I reached the sign pointing south, across the valley to the farm, and that looked a mess too. It seemed, from the sign, that the farm might have a camping barn or it might not, but there was no mention of my preferred options: a bunkhouse or a camping site.

The obvious thing to do was to walk across to the farm and take a look at it. I paused and looked down the valley and then up to the farm on the hill beyond it. I *could* walk down and then up to get there, and it might be very nice when I arrived, or I could go on and invest that distance and effort to take me further along the Coast to Coast Walk. If they were serious, I reasoned, the Coast to Coast should provide most of their custom and they'd want to show a professional face towards walkers. The fact that they didn't, spoke volumes.

The idea of a proper bed had taken root in my mind. I knew there was a hostel in the next town, Kirkby Stephen, so I got my phone out and rang them. No answer. I left a message telling them I was on my way and I'd like a bed, then I left Bents Farm behind me and made some more forward progress.

I'd already done a full day's walking and the pull to Kirkby Stephen was hard work. The daylight was starting to fade and so was I.

At Smardale Bridge, I crossed Smardale Beck and walked around the head of Smardale Gill. Across the gill, I could see the old limestone quarries and the lime kilns which used to

43

produce quicklime for building and agriculture, together with the railway viaduct which was built in 1861 to transport the finished product.

After what seemed like a very long walk but which, in reality, was no more than a few kilometres, I was striding across fields, keen to get to the hostel as soon as I could in case it was busy.

I passed underneath the Settle to Carlisle railway line and there was Kirkby Stephen below me. I skirted the Iron Age hillfort of Croglam Castle and I was in the town.

Kirkby Stephen was the first town of any reasonable size that I'd passed on my walk. As I strolled down the main street, it felt as if I'd returned to civilisation after a long absence. There were cars and shops, post boxes and street lamps, and a total absence of cows and sheep. Which all goes to show that everything is relative: the population of Kirkby Stephen is less than 2,000 people, so it's not quite the bustling metropolis it seemed to me at the time.

The hostel was easy to find, although the building looked unlikely because it was clearly an old Methodist church. It was built from local stone, with what looked like Bath stone on the corners and around the doors and the stained-glass windows.

I followed the signs down a side passage and knocked on a door which had a combination lock, and a white envelope sellotaped to it. No answer. I tried the handle and found the door was locked. The envelope stuck to the door was addressed to "Phil". I didn't know who Phil was and I wondered if I should open it.

I knocked again, harder this time, but there was still no response.

Maybe the letter was for me and they'd got the name wrong? Or maybe someone called Phil was booked in at the hostel and the letter contained instructions for him. If the envelope wasn't for me, then I didn't want to open it. I felt that to do so would be to betray the trust which someone had shown in passers-by when they stuck it on the door. Guessing whether or not the letter was intended for me was getting me nowhere, so

I started thinking about the consequences of opening it. If it turned out to be for me, well then, no harm done. If it was for someone else, I might glean from it how to gain access to the hostel and I could always stick it back on the door for Phil after I'd read it.

Working on the basis that it's usually easier to ask for forgiveness than it is to get permission, I pulled the envelope off the door and ripped open the flap.

Inside was a note, providing Phil with the combination number to gain access and asking him to call a mobile phone number.

I typed in the number, opened the door and called out, "Hello?"

There was no answer, so I went in. Through a small foyer full of wellington boots, to a second door, which I opened. As I did so, I heard a door click open on the far side of the old church.

"Hello?" slightly louder this time.

Still nothing.

I stopped and listened. I was in what had been the minister's part of the church; backstage, if you will. The inside was exactly what you'd expect of a nonconformist church built in the second half of the nineteenth century: Stained, varnished wood, occasional stained glass and the odd memorial tablet to some local worthy who had more social standing than the rest.

Then another door click from the other side of the church made me jump.

I headed straight for it and opened the door, maybe a trifle quicker than was strictly necessary.

Still nothing.

I realised that appearances can have a big impact: I'd started thinking of this place as a church because it looked exactly like one, even though I knew it was now a hostel.

I decided to apply some "system" and I methodically went through every room which was not locked in the whole of the building. I found bunk rooms, shower rooms, toilets, a kitchen and a lounge. The main body of the church still held stained wooden pews and a piano. But I didn't find any people.

I also discovered that the building was an airlock. When I opened one door another, which didn't close properly, on the other side of the church, clicked open. Then, some thirty seconds later, and because it was fitted with an automatic door closer, it clicked again as it almost closed.

Making a mental note to refresh my memory of the story of the *Marie Celeste* when I got home, I stuck Phil's note back on the outside door and carried my stuff through to a bunk.

I phoned the number in Phil's letter but got no reply, so I showered and prepared my dinner. I was doing my washing up when the owners arrived, and I was able to introduce myself and pay. They were still expecting Phil when I went to bed but he never showed.

I slept like a log in the old church and when I rose the next morning I found that I was the only resident in the hostel. I shaved, got organised, got dressed and then got organised some more. I carefully and deliberately worked through a stretching routine and then, felling quite chipper, I went through to the dining area and got some breakfast.

It was 8am on a Sunday morning when I left and Kirkby Stephen was still slunk in idle Sabbath-day slumber. Through the quiet streets I walked, past the little stone houses, through the back-streets to the River Eden and over the old stone bridge. A heron stood in midstream, weight on one leg, the other bent, one beady eye watching me as I crossed the old bridge.

A signpost on the east bank told me that I'd walked 82 miles and I still had another 108 to go. I climbed uphill along a quiet lane and edged around the big quarry at Hartley. I felt optimistic for two reasons: firstly, today I should reach the halfway point on the walk, at Keld; and secondly, and just as important in morale terms, I would walk off the edge of my first map and onto my second and final map.

Ahead of me, up on the skyline, I could see the dark points of Nine Standards Rigg. The Nine Standards are nine stone cairns, built on the summit of the fell. Strange as it seems, no-one knows how old they are, nor why they were built. That they have been there for many centuries seems certain, but we can only speculate about why someone went to the effort of constructing and maintaining them. Were they a boundary marker? Or were they, as some like to believe, made to look like the tents of an English army, erected to deter the marauding Scots? Whatever the reason, they make a striking skyline.

Up Faraday Gill towards Nine Standards the path diverges and there are three routes to choose from, or any number if you like to forge your own.

An incident happened during my Coast to Coast Walk which I'm going to insert at this point in my narrative. I'm not going to disclose the location, nor any information from which the location could be calculated, for reasons which will become clear.

I was in a light-hearted mood, with nothing on my mind but my hat, when I heard a squeaking noise, not dissimilar to a dog's chew-toy. It quickly got louder and there was a rush of air as something swooped past my head, travelling at a great rate of knots. I ducked to the ground, almost as a reflex, and I saw a grey bird with black wing-tips soaring back up into the sky and begin circling, as if preparing for another pass. But he was merely the decoy. As I watched my aggressor, a second bird rocketed down and past me, making the same loud squeaking sound.

I dropped onto one knee and waved my trekking poles over my head to prevent them from getting too close, while I looked quickly around me to work out what the hell was going on.

The second bird was a dull brown and, for that reason, seemed to be a different species. For a moment I wondered if they'd started to cooperate as they did in Alfred Hitchcock's film, *The Birds*. Both birds kept up their squeaking and flew one each side of me, making it impossible to watch both of them at the same time. They were obviously working in tandem, because if I watched one of them for too long, the other swooped in and *vice versa*.

Something had clearly upset them and I got the distinct

impression that thing was a big bloke with a rucksack. My first reaction was what you might expect of *Homo sapiens,* the ape which developed out of the savannah to inhabit the world: to fight with them and to assert my right to walk across the moor. As the species at the top of the food chain, I was not going to be pushed about by a couple of birds. But after a split second my rational brain started working and I realised that they were unlikely to hurt me, and that it was all but impossible for me to fight them. I'd probably strayed near their young or onto their hunting ground, or something else that mattered deeply to birds. The best thing I could do, I reasoned, was to clear off out of it.

So I kept my hat on as a final line of defence, waved my trekking poles over my head to stop the birds getting too near me, and swore at them when they tried, partly to deter them and partly to vent my frustration. They were persistent, I'll say that for them. I checked the map afterwards and they kept up their sorties for over a kilometre of walking. That's a good fifteen minutes.

I did some research when I got home and discovered the birds were hen harriers. Although they are legally protected, hen harriers do not fit into the business plans of the major grouse-shooting estates and they are ruthlessly persecuted by landowners and gamekeepers. As a result, hen harriers are almost extinct in England, which is why their location on this walk must remain a mystery. One website even had a recording of their distinctive squeaking sound. I pressed *play* and my girlfriend laughed as I visibly jumped at the sound, and goose bumps formed on my arms.

The main charity for the protection of birds in the UK is the RSPB, the Royal Society for the Protection of Birds. After my walk, I gave the RSPB the exact location of the hen harriers but received only a polite acknowledgement. No action on the Riggindale eagle and no effective action on the hen harrier. The RSPB might need a change of name.

My map showed a bunkhouse in Keld but, when I got there, there was no trace of it. It didn't worry me unduly: it was a nice afternoon and the campsite at Park House looked ideal. Sheltered and flat, with short grass and clean showers and toilets. The campsite owner tried hard to talk me into renting a yurt, but I pointed out that I hadn't carried my tent up hill and down dale merely to sit in a yurt and look at it.

I pitched in the lee of a hedge while the disappointed proprietor made her way back to the farmhouse. The sun was strong and my laundry dried quickly, so I tucked it away and walked the mile into Keld to use their telephone box.

Keld is a pleasant little village. At the height of the lead mining industry in the late 1800s, its population numbered over 6,000. Now around 100 people live here. I couldn't tell whether the old Methodist church was boarded up because people were no longer religious or because there just aren't enough people in Keld to fill it any more.

A telephone chat with my girlfriend put a spring in my step and I enjoyed the walk back along the quiet lane in the late afternoon sunshine.

When I got back to the campsite I found I was no longer alone: a second yurt-shunner was putting up a hiking tent under the hedge. Also a coast-to-coaster, Rob was carrying a large day sack and was having an even bigger rucksack sent on ahead each day by van. He'd started out carrying everything, he told me, but was done in after the first day. He had almost decided to give up the walk, but his wife suggested baggage transfer and had paid for the courier service as a present. It didn't seem to have occurred to either of them to carry fewer things or to get some lightweight kit. Rob was still walking though, and I guess that's what matters in the end.

In the space of that short conversation, the sky had clouded over and now rain started coming down. I wished my load-bearing friend well and headed to the campsite kitchen to prepare my dinner.

In the kitchen, I found two women busily at work. They were mother and daughter, walking part of the Pennine Way together. We ate in the dark kitchen and then nursed mugs of tea as we watched the rain falling outside, through the open door. One of the ladies was not impressed with the weather and said so. My breezy southern retort, "If you can't take a joke, you shouldn't live up north", pretty much ended the evening and we parted to go to our different tents.

The rain eased to a thick drizzle, but with a dark sky behind it. In my tent, I perused my map and wondered what tomorrow would bring.

I left the yurts of Keld at breakfast-time next morning. I'd spent a chilly night, which had necessitated getting up to put on all my spare clothing, and I'd been kept awake in the early hours of the morning by two owls hunting in the moonlight, but that's the sort of awake I don't mind being kept, if you see what I mean.

It was a grey, misty morning and I couldn't work out which way the weather might go. Greyer and wetter? Or would the sun come out and burn it off? Either way I felt pretty good. I was clean and my clothes were clean, I had plenty of food and I was over halfway on my journey to the North Sea. It would take more than a bit of weather to dampen my spirits.

I had options from Keld to Reeth. I could go up high, over the moors and through the old mine workings, or I could follow the river and walk down through Swaledale. The high route was tempting. I'd be able to see for miles if the weather was good, and there's always something atmospheric about industrial sites abandoned in the 1700s and 1800s. Swaledale, on the other hand, was equally enticing. It would look good whatever the weather but at this time of year, springtime, it would be a mass of wild flowers.

I decided to follow the River Swale.

I started by climbing Birk Hill. At this point my route was coterminous with the Pennine Way, another long-distance path on my To Do list, and it also coincided with a third walk, one so eloquently described by Wainwright in one of my favourite books, *A Pennine Journey.*

The morning warmed nicely as I puffed my way up Birk Hill and contoured around the hillside above Rukin Wood. As I

50

strolled along the open hill, the sun came out in earnest and the mist began to lift. I saw the ruins of Crackpot Hall across the valley, and behind it the old lead workings. Along the valley floor I could see the Swale winding through flat, green pastures, divided up by dry stone walls as the valley stretched away towards Richmond, out of sight over the horizon.

Below me, Swaledale was clear, and the mist had risen and concentrated to form a thin band of white cloud, roughly at the level of the surrounding hilltops. Above that was a bright, blue, sunny sky. I realised that either route option, high or low, would be stunning in this weather.

I was about 250m above the Swale and I needed to get to the riverside path, so I made my way to the end of Kisdon, the hill I was traversing, and dropped down to Muker.

From Muker I had to double back on myself, heading upstream to the little footbridge over the Swale. Once on the north bank, I started walking eastwards on the thin, stony path between the steep hillside (to my left) and a barbed wire fence (to my right).

Down here, I was on the floodplain of the River Swale, which was quietly gurgling away over the rocks, only taking up about a quarter of its channel. I tried to imagine it in spate.

Swaledale was undeniably beautiful and the going, as racing folk say, was good, so I made creditable progress. Banks of bluebells peeped out from the wooded stretches and the trees were in full leaf.

I reached Ivelet Bridge, a pack-horse bridge dating from the late 1500s, and let myself through the small gate in the field wall to reach the lane.

A large stone set into the verge here is supposed to be a coffin stone, that is, a spot where pall-bearers could place the coffin they were carrying without getting it dirty as they rested.

In late-medieval times, England experienced a population increase. More settlements were built, often with churches, but the older churches carefully guarded their right to conduct burials (and, of course, by doing so they safeguarded the income which accrued from those burials). If you lived in a village where the church had no burial rights, you might have to travel considerable distances to bury your dead. This led to the establishment of "corpse roads", tracks from villages in which the church had no burial rights leading to places where the dead could lawfully be interred. In this case the coffin stone is on the old corpse road from Muker to St Andrew's Church in Grinton, 16 miles down the dale. In those days, St Andrew's was the only church in upper Swaledale permitted to conduct burials.

Soon I was in Gunnerside, looking for The Kings Arms, which my researches had indicated could supply me with food and drink. I found the pub with no difficulty and it looked enticing with tables and benches set out in front of it in the sunshine, but it was firmly locked up with a large *For Sale* sign fixed to the front of it.

I sat on one of the benches and dug out my route notes to work out what else might be available, when my friend from Keld with the large rucksack walked around the corner of the pub. Just a little way up the street, he told me, was a café which was already serving lunch.

I found it without any problem. From the outside, the establishment looked as if it was aimed at elderly coach parties and the inside only served to reinforce this impression: all lace curtains, doilies and fussy knick-knacks. I wondered how they'd take to a grubby hiker, especially if they thought I might act as a deterrent to the elderly cake-enthusiast who formed their target demographic, but they treated me well enough and I enjoyed my lunch.

Full up and rested, I wandered down the silent old streets in the sunshine, back towards the path across the fields. The trail was clearly marked by being mown from the grass and wildflowers which filled each field. And what wild flowers they were! Miles and miles of hazy yellow gauze across the green grass.

My route was crossed by dry stone walls at frequent intervals, each with a little wooden gate where the path went through it. These gates we clearly made for people of smaller stature than me, and without rucksacks, for I had to hop and lever myself through almost all of them.

Every field seemed to have a stone barn that looked as if it dated from the Great Rebuilding, that period in the 1600s when improved economic conditions in England allowed the replacement of many timber buildings with longer-lasting stone ones.

Rather than group their animals and feed in barns adjoining the farmhouse in winter, Dales farmers found it more efficient to site their barns in the fields. The stone barns I was passing were used to house the hay crop, each one storing the crop produced from the field in which the barn is located. In winter, cattle were kept inside the barn and fed on the hay already stored in it. Their manure was used to fertilise the field outside and thus facilitate the next year's hay crop.

I stopped to take on fluid at Reeth, in The Buck Inn, and I was sitting outside at a table when three men arrived. They were all Coast to Coast walkers, with their baggage being sent ahead by courier service. And The Buck Inn was their destination for the day! I finished quickly and moved on before I lost the will to walk.

As I wandered on down Swaledale, I pondered the lot of the non-camper. It was 3pm when I'd left The Buck. For those guys, the day was over and all that awaited them was a few hours to kill before they could go into the bar for dinner and drinks. I could fit in a lot of miles before bed or, if I chose, just a few. They had no such choice: they could only kill time until dinner. As if that weren't enough, next morning I would have put even more miles on the clock, and during the best part of the day, before they even left the pub.

I could have killed them from jealousy of their hot showers, cooked dinner and the convivial evening they had ahead of them in the bar, but I was glad that my itinerary was decided by me, as I walked it, and not by some tour company in an office in London.

I kept reminding myself of that as I plodded the next 9km through the long, hot afternoon towards Richmond.

My path became paved with stone flags, and it wasn't long before these flagstones became the coping stones on a field wall and I was walking on top of that wall, a few metres above the river. It was an odd, Alice-in-Wonderland sensation, and slightly precarious in places, but a very practical way to route the path because it would be still usable when the river is high, in winter.

The wall dipped back down to the riverside, and I walked along a grass embankment and over some large stepping stones which enabled me to cross a tributary stream. Up on the hilltops to my left I could see the scars of the old lead-mining industry.

There is evidence of lead mining going back to Roman times in Yorkshire, but demand for lead increased significantly after the Norman Conquest as the great cathedrals and castles were built. Production was high and it was said that lead from Yorkshire was used on the rooves at Windsor Castle, St Peter's in Rome and even on churches in Jerusalem.

At first, bell pits were dug and they can still be seen as lines of circular depressions on the landscape, where miners dug small chambers at different points along a vein of lead ore.

Hushing was used extensively, especially on steep hillsides. Streams were dammed and when sufficient water had built up, it was released to scour the hillside clear of earth and expose the ore. The scarring caused by hushing is still very evident around Gunnerside.

When the simpler methods of extraction, such as bell pits and hushing, had delivered all they could, levels were dug into the hillsides to get at the lead ore. The entrances to these mines and the old mine buildings are still visible, and their spoil heaps stand out due to their lack of vegetation because of the spoil's high lead content.

The industry's heyday was in the eighteenth and nineteenth centuries, when Britain became the world's pre-eminent lead-producer, and the population of Swaledale surged as a result.

By the late 1800s the industry was in decline because of cheap foreign imports and people began to move away from

Swaledale. The last working mine here closed in 1912.

It would be easy to criticise the people who operated the mines in Swaledale because of the mess they left behind, but most of them were doing dirty, dangerous work for very little money. Life was so hard that many miners and their families grew vegetables and knitted clothes to supplement their income from mining. The casualty rate must have been dreadful by modern standards: the average lifespan of a miner in the 1860s was 45. As late as 1872 the rules of one Swaledale mine dictated that children aged 12-16 years were "only" permitted to work 54 hours a week.

According to the United States Geological Survey, the UK is now only the 35th largest lead producer in the world, very near the bottom of the table. China holds the top spot, producing more than twice as much as its nearest rival. I wondered how current working conditions in Chinese lead production compare with those of Swaledale in its heyday.

In the distance I could see the tower of Marrick Priory, a Benedictine nunnery established in the 1100s, and soon I was able to look down on it from the footpath leading up to Steps Wood.

Like Shap Abbey, Marrick Priory survived the first few years of the Dissolution of the Monasteries, but in 1540 the Abbess and her sixteen nuns were evicted and pensioned off, and the priory became the property of the Crown. In 1970 it was converted into an outdoor education centre for young people.

My path took me away from Marrick Priory and away from the River Swale, across undulating fields of deep green pasture. I passed beneath the cliff face of Applegarth Scar and knew I was close to the camping barn at East Applegarth Farm, a few miles west of Richmond. It had been a long day and I decided to call time and try to get a bed for the night.

There was plenty of room at the camping barn, because the only other occupant was my old mucker from Keld: Rob with the very big rucksack. The beds were converted cattle stalls in an old byre but the shower was modern, clean and hot.

Tomorrow would be Day 8 and I felt I was due a rest day, but there was nothing to occupy me at East Applegate. I had a food parcel waiting for me in Richmond Post Office so I decided that tomorrow I'd collect it, have a lazy day in Richmond and then walk the short distance to Brompton-on-Swale.

I was woken up in the early morning by the wind howling around the outside of the barn. I lay in my sleeping bag and wondered what on earth the weather would be like when I got up. By the time I dragged myself out of bed, the wind had dropped and in its place a thick fog swirled around the farm. I peered out into the gloom. It didn't matter too much: I wasn't likely to lose my way between here and Richmond.

Rob announced his intention to walk to Danby Wiske, 25km away. No rest day for him.

Chapter 4

The Vale of Mowbray

A castle unslighted, civic pride, the pub that never opens and a rest day ruined.

I soon covered the short distance to Richmond and celebrated my return to civilisation by popping into a coffee shop on Richmond's market place, one of the biggest in England (the market place, not the coffee shop). I was in no hurry to claim my food parcel: once I'd collected it, I'd have to carry it, so I finished my coffee and went into Richmond Castle, its only visitor on a grey, misty morning.

The town of Richmond was established by the Normans in 1071 and the castle was completed in 1086. Built to help control the north of England, Richmond Castle sits on a commanding site overlooking the River Swale and it was never damaged by war or slighting, so it's still an imposing sight. From 1908-1910 the garrison commander at the castle was Robert Baden-Powell, founder of the Boy Scouts, and during the First World War a group of conscientious objectors were imprisoned here.

The town was grey and quiet when I came back out of the castle gate. Like any town, after you've been out in the wilds for a few days, Richmond felt bigger than it actually was. The last census records a population of just 8,413.

Richmond is a lovely place. I expect its residents are

proud of their town and justifiably so. 8,412 of them were able to keep their civic pride to themselves, but it was too much for the 8,413th. I was walking across the market place towards the post office, where four days' worth of neatly parcelled camping food was waiting for me, when I was accosted (that's the only way I can describe it) by a lady aged about 50, wearing a black coat. She saw me, turned from her route across the market place to head straight for me, and engaged me without any preamble or explanation.

"You really ought to try the Castle Walk, it starts just down there," she pointed over my left shoulder, "It's lovely."

I looked around myself to see who she was talking to and realised with a jolt that it was me. Expecting some sort of follow-up along the lines of breakdown insurance or religion, I groped for a suitable response.

"Oh, er, thank you."

If she noticed my confusion or my reserve, she gave no sign of it.

"It's a beautiful town and you get some lovely views from the Castle Walk. Just down there, past that shop."

She stood there smiling, as if waiting for me to toddle off in the direction indicated, like a good chap.

"Thank you. Just down there?" I glanced in the direction she'd specified, to demonstrate that I understood. "Right-ho, I'll definitely give it a go."

"If you like walking, you'll love it." She beamed at me, clearly expecting that her enthusiastic endorsement of the Castle Walk would cause me to push off towards it without further ado.

When I'm ambushed in conversational terms, I may not be able to summon up a wit equivalent to that of Oscar Wilde, but I'm *always* resistant to being jollied along. Never jolly me. I pointed in the opposite direction, to the post office.

"Just got to go to the post office first. I've got to pick up a parcel."

I smiled to show her that her work here was done and she could now leave me alone. Her smile faded a touch and I felt like a bully. Goodness knows why – it wasn't me who was pestering a total stranger with walks around the castle.

"But I'll definitely take a look at Castle Walk. Thank you. Thanks very much."

I edged around her and headed for the post office, reflecting as I did so that it was good that people were proud of their town, but it would be nicer still if they waited to be introduced before extolling its virtues to complete strangers. And that made me cross with myself because it sounded like something a character in a Jane Austen novel might say. The fact that my tolerance level was that of a Regency spinster was too much to contemplate, so my mind sought other literary allusions to divert itself from too much self-examination as I hurried to the post office.

"A modicum of municipal pride might be considered beneficial; an excess of it, vexatious." And if Samuel Johnson didn't say that, well, he should have.

I was wondering how Shakespeare might have put it, when I reached the post office and gave the thing up.

The post office staff were courteous and efficient, and before long I was back out into the market place, hugging a brown paper parcel and looking for a seat to unwrap it, free from interference by well-meaning natives.

With my new food safely stowed away, I thought about what I'd do with my rest day in Richmond. In the absence of any other ideas, I decided to take a stroll around Castle Walk. Why not? It came highly recommended.

Richmond is a pleasant town, with history and character, and the Castle Walk had both, in spades. It turned out to be a short promenade walk around the base of the castle's outer wall, with railings to protect walkers from the drop down to the Swale below. The mist still hung about, under a white sky, and the trees looked impossibly green. I was the only person on Castle Walk and I enjoyed it so much that I went round twice.

That done, I got some lunch in a pub and had a think about the afternoon. I seemed to have pretty much exhausted the attractions of Richmond. I knew there was no campsite or hostel in the town, so I'd have to walk on at least a few kilometres.   Brompton-on-Swale had a hostel and was sufficiently remote that I could wander on a little way and camp if the hostel was full. Brompton was another 7km.

I was about halfway to Brompton-on-Swale when it occurred to me that I'd cocked up my rest day. Far from "resting", I'd put my rucksack on and wandered around Richmond all morning, before adding 4kg of food to it, wandering about some more and then setting off for Brompton. My feet were telling me that walking with a rucksack all day did not constitute a rest and my brain agreed. It was simply what I'd been doing since Day 1.

The distance to Brompton was increased significantly by an unsympathetic footpath diversion which, for the most part, routed the Coast to Coast along a busy "A" road. The hurtling lorries and cars were an assault on the senses as I plodded towards Catterick Race Course. I had to dice with death to cross the road at Catterick Bridge because I'd missed the final part of the diversion, but after dodging in and out of cones and lorries, knocking over a sign and vaulting a barrier, I regained the path alive, albeit in the grotty end of Brompton.

I padded through roadworks and industrial estates, and then into the village. The hostel was easy to find and I was given a spare bed in a dormitory already occupied by two ex-military men who were taking a canoeing course nearby. They were sociable types and the meeting led to a convivial evening in the pub a few doors down.

When I got back from the pub, I lay in my bunk and pondered what had become of my rest day. I'd walked 14km with my pack at its heaviest because of the food parcel, and that didn't include my perambulations around Richmond. I felt as if I still owed myself a rest day. But that meant, if today was a walking day, that I should be much further along the trail. 14km wasn't much forward progress for a full day of walking. Any way I looked at it, the day seemed a bit of a dud. I tried to take the big view: I'd walked 191km so far with only 118km still to do. I'd had so much good weather that there must be bad weather coming soon; I had four days' worth of food in my pack and no blisters.   With no return rail ticket, I wasn't on a deadline, so I could slot in another rest day whenever I felt like it, or the occasional short distance day if I preferred.   Put like that, I couldn't see much wrong with my situation.

I slept well and made an early start the next morning, walking along lanes and across cattle pastures. The going was easy, especially so when compared to the Lake District and the Pennines, and for the most part my path was dry and level. Overhead, the sky had that "big sky" feel that you get when you walk across a large, flat area, with patches of blue between white, fluffy clouds coming in slowly from the west.

I reached Danby Wiske at 11am.

Danby Wiske is the lowest inland point on the walk, physically because it stands only 35m above sea level and psychologically because its only pub never seems to open. With all the promise of a mirage showing an oasis in the desert, it looks to be a fully functioning pub, but it wasn't open when I knocked on its door and it wasn't open when television presenter Julia Bradbury passed through, making her BBC TV documentary on the Coast to Coast Walk. It wasn't open for Wainwright either, so good luck if you ever develop a thirst in Danby Wiske.

Apart from the mirage of a pub, Danby's only other claim to fame is that it was the home of George Calvert, Lord Baltimore, the founder of the state of Maryland in the American colonies. A long way to go for a drink perhaps, but if your local won't open, what can you do?

I decided to make for Osmotherley. Once there I'd camp or go into brick depending on what was available, the weather and how I felt. I struck on out of Danby, glad of the occasional shade provided by clouds and trees as the day warmed up. On the far horizon I could see a long, dark bar which my map told me was the North York Moors.

The day got hotter and I wished I'd packed more water. Down here on the lowlands there wasn't the opportunity to get clean water from streams as I'd been able to in the hills, so what

I was carrying was all that was available.

The A19 road was a real shock. I approached it by a small lane which joined it at a crossroads and I stood on the verge for a few seconds to take it all in. A dual carriageway with four lanes of traffic travelling at maximum speed. Filter lanes for the crossroads made it, in effect, a six lane highway. And it was busy: heavy lorries, vans and cars streamed past without a break. I remembered a driving instructor telling me that, "Most people are poor judges of speed, time and distance". "Speed, time and distance" seemed the critical factors here and I realised that crossing would require some thought, particularly if me and most of the motorists were prone to errors of judgement.

After a few minutes, I'd developed a plan to reduce this monster road-crossing into smaller, more manageable component parts. I walked down the side of the carriageway until I was past the filter lanes. I'd now cut six lanes down to four, because I'd cut out the two filter lanes. If I crossed one carriageway at a time and used the central reservation as a refuge, I'd shrink the problem into two smaller road crossings.

I did a couple of practice sprints up and down the verge, to make sure that, despite the weight of my rucksack, my legs could be relied upon to accelerate when I needed them. Then I waited for my first break in the traffic and went for it.

I reached the other side in one piece and without any car horns sounding, so I counted that a success. Never mind wading rivers on the Appalachian Trail, I felt. Those American johnnies should try to cross the A19! Why the council don't put a footbridge or an underpass there is beyond me. Maybe it's cheaper to scrape hikers off lorries at the next services.

I passed quickly through Ingleby Arncliffe and reached Ingleby Cross to find its only pub was shut and wouldn't open for another hour. The pub had a sign up, informing punters that they allow camping, an idea which greatly tempted me after a day's walking, but an hour is a long time to hang about and I knew I could easily make Osmotherley if I kept on going.

The last part of my day's walk was steep, up gravel

forestry tracks through South Wood. High trees shaded my path, leaving hot patches of full sun where the branches didn't extend far enough to create shade on the track. I kept my eyes peeled for a glimpse of Mount Grace Priory, which should have been just to the south-west of me, but I never saw hide nor hair of it. I wasn't inclined to go in search of it because that would involve losing height, and so create the need to regain it again.

The drive to keep on walking can sometimes wane a little in late afternoon. After all,

"A poor life this if, full of care,

We have no time to stand and stare."[7]

I paused to look back across the Vale of Mowbray which I'd just crossed. A patchwork of fields and hedgerows as far as the eye could see, the whole thing topped off with a false ceiling of white-grey cloud. I tried to pick out Richmond, on the far side of the vale, but it was simply too far away. That fact made me feel I'd walked a good distance and I turned and followed the track into Osmotherley.

I turned onto the lane leading out of the village and soon found the hostel I was looking for. It's a picturesque place, an old red-brick mill which has been converted from industrial use into accommodation. The mill race and the site of the old water wheel are still very obvious, but I could see no trace of the building's function as a dance hall between the wars. I wondered what romances had started and ended here.

As I waited for the hostel's reception to open, I chatted with two local men, one of whom told me they were "Doing the Coast to Coast backwards". His friend picked up on the potential for a joke at about the same time I did and quickly explained that his colleague meant they were walking the Coast to Coast Walk from east to west, not actually walking backwards (a concept they both found very amusing). Being local, they knew the area well and they told me about a path under Kirby Bank which, they reckoned, would take an hour off my walk tomorrow if the weather was bad. And bad it would be, one of

---

[7] From the poem *Leisure* by W. H. Davies.

them went on: heavy rain was forecast for the next day. He leaned towards me as if to emphasise his point, and said it again.

"Heavy rain." He paused, as if for still more emphasis. "All day."

I made small talk with the hostel receptionist as I checked in. He started filling out a form, looked up at me, and commented, "You've been lucky, haven't you?"

I thought about it, but I couldn't see how I'd been "lucky". I hadn't won the lottery, nor had I been kidnapped by a busload of bikini models, and I'd reached Osmotherley by my own effort and ingenuity. On the other hand, as far as I knew, I didn't have any serious illnesses. I passed it back to him.

"How do you mean?"

He looked up from his form.

"You've had good weather. It's going to tip it down tomorrow. Torrential rain." He leaned forward and made eye contact, as if to underline his point, like the man on the hostel steps. "All day."

I had a sudden flash of inspiration.

"Let's make it two nights".

Which is how I came to be taking a real rest day in Osmotherley.

Chapter 5

The North York Moors

A rest day taken, the pain of half a book, friends in the fog, the invention of the whiskey mattress, three Yorkshiremen; a mine, a folly and a waterfall.

Once the decision was made and the extra night's bed was booked, I found I was surprisingly relaxed about the prospect of making no forward progress for a day. It would, I felt, be the perfect opportunity to recharge my batteries, metaphorically in my case but literally in the case of my phone and my camera, and I could do some laundry and check over my kit. By the time I left, I decided, both my gear and I would be in tip-top condition for the push to the east coast.

I ate a sociable dinner in the communal kitchen with two retired teachers from Cornwall and a couple from Amsterdam then, after everyone had gone to bed, I sneaked back down in my underpants and washed my walking trousers in the kitchen sink. I soon had them hanging up in the drying room with my tent, socks and underpants, to dry.

I don't carry much in the way of spare clothes when I'm walking. A spare pair of socks are always useful; if I'm away for more than a week, maybe a set of spare underpants and a shirt as well. I don't begrudge carrying these items when they're clean, but my attitude towards them changes when they need washing. That fact alone transforms them from useful items into mere passengers in my rucksack, and I don't like carrying ballast.

So it was with the sense of a job well done that I went to bed that evening, in a six-bed dorm all to myself, with my own toilet and shower. I slept like a log and was woken in the early hours by rain hammering on the windows. I groaned and then felt quite bright when I remembered that I wouldn't be walking in it: today was my rest day.

I got out of bed and pulled back the blind, solely to see the bad weather I wouldn't be walking in, to enjoy it more fully, you might say. The early-morning sky was an overpowering dark grey and rain was lashing down, driving hard as if it's one purpose was to batter the ground into submission. I got back under my warm duvet and let the weather get on with it.

Confined by the weather and with a second night booked, I had little choice but to take a proper rest day. I did some stretches, carefully and thoroughly, and then sneaked down to the drying room in my underpants, put my trousers back on and retrieved my tent, my shirt, my pants and my socks.

Next, I studied my map over a quiet coffee in the hostel's lounge. There were still 88km to be walked before I'd get to Robin Hood's Bay, or between two and three days if I reckoned in terms of time rather than distance. The Lion Inn at Blakey allowed coast-to-coasters to camp and looked a good stopping point, as did Priory Farm, just before Grosmont. Time to get organised.

Back in my room, I emptied my rucksack, laid out my food on the bed and looked at it for a few seconds. At least I wouldn't be going hungry. I divided the food into three separate days' rations, then took the little that was left over downstairs to the kitchen and left it there for other travellers.

I carefully repacked my rucksack. All I needed was another night's sleep and I was ready to go. The rain was still driving down, so the sights of Osmotherley would have to wait until another day.

Back in the lounge, I selected a book from their surprisingly comprehensive bookshelf and settled down with my feet up to read through the afternoon, the rain still hammering against the windows. By teatime I was halfway through my book, but it was time to put it back. As I did so I realised that, even though I'd enjoyed the first half, I'll never discover how that book finishes. To do so, I'd have to buy a copy, and I can't bring myself to pay full price for a book when I only want to read the second half of it. The odds are not great, but if you happen to have the second half of *44, Scotland Street,* and you're wondering what to do with half a book, get in touch.

That evening I set my alarm for 5.30 the next morning, but I was awake and up before the alarm could go off.

No-one else was up, so I breakfasted alone in the hostel kitchen, left my key on the counter and started out.

There was no doubt in my mind that the rest day had done me some good. I could feel it in my legs and my mind felt sharper. I thought about it as I walked, concerned that I'd felt guilty about not making any forward progress and that it had taken the threat of foul weather to push me into resting for a day. The benefits were obvious, but were never going to be realised until I could ignore the drive to walk on.

I filed that piece of learning away for my next walk and paused to check my route on the map. I was about to walk along the northern edge of the Cleveland Hills and across the North York Moors. The rain was intermittent but the fog was closing in, and by the time I reached Lord Stones, visibility was down to about 10m.

I remembered the advice I'd been given yesterday, about the short cut around the base of Kirby Bank, but when I got to the point where the path divides, I didn't like the look of it. That unmarked path might be easy to follow. Or it might not. There was no telling from where I stood and it would be easy to get lost up here, especially in such thick fog. My original path, however, coincided with the Cleveland Way for the next few miles and the Cleveland Way was marked and signed. It might take a bit longer and there might be more up and down, but if I stayed on my planned route I could follow the signs and be sure of getting where I wanted to go, fog or no fog.

Also at the base of Kirby Bank, and also contemplating whether to take the high road or the low road, were a man and a small terrier-like dog, Mike and Alfie. Mike and I discussed the relative merits of both routes while Alfie sniffed my shoes. No matter how much talking we did, there would still be walking to do, so I set off up the steep hill right in front of us, while Mike and Alfie took the lower route, through the trees to our left.

There must, I calculated, be superb views from these hills in good weather. As it was, all I could see in any direction was a few heather bushes. Just to add to the jollity of the occasion, the rain had picked up and the wind was driving it horizontally across the moor. I put more clothing on, cinched down my hood and gloves, and squelched on.

It would be very easy to get very lost up here, particularly in thick fog, even though help might not be far away. As I walked, my mind wandered away on routes of its own, thinking about instances where people had assumed they were in danger when they weren't. I remembered the story of a Fleet Air Arm pilot, shot down into the sea during the attack on the Italian fleet at Taranto in 1940. He described trying to swim for the shore and safety, until he was too tired to swim any more. That was when he put his feet down and found he'd been swimming for his life in three feet of water. Things aren't always as bad as we think they are.

I pulled my attention back to the present and checked my watch. I wouldn't be able to fix my position by landmarks or by compass in the fog, but I knew roughly how fast I walked, so it was important to keep track of time from a known point.

Colossal stones loomed over me in the murk and I realised that I'd arrived at another known point: the Wain Stones. From here, the North York Moors National Park leaflet had promised me, "Some of the most spectacular views in the whole National Park", but the fog was so thick that I could just about see my own feet. At least, I think they were my feet. I wiggled one of them just to make sure.

The Wain Stones are supposed to have Bronze Age "cup and ring" carvings on them, but I didn't know where they were on the stones and I didn't feel any urge to start grubbing about in an attempt to find them[8].

I checked my map and my watch again. In about 15 minutes I should come down from the hills, cross a "B" road and then climb back up onto the moors again. Completely indifferent to my calculations, the rain pelted down.

I crossed the "B" road at Clay Bank and starting climbing up onto Carr Ridge. The fog created a strange, slightly claustrophobic feeling as I walked. No matter how much progress I made, it was as if I was permanently surrounded by four walls: to the front and rear, and to the sides, each just a few feet away from me. I was out on the open hill, but I would have felt less confined if I'd spent the whole day in my spare bedroom at home.

There was a stone seat on the top of Round Hill and I took it. The insoles inside my sodden shoes had slipped about and folded under themselves, creating a concertina effect which was most uncomfortable underfoot. I shrugged off my pack and removed my gaiters and shoes to get at the insoles. With a bit of effort, I got them straightened out again and put the shoes and gaiters back on.

The next few kilometres to Bloworth Crossing were along a gravel track that had water either running across it or standing on it in deep puddles for most of the way. The water caused my insoles to slide and concertina, again and again. When they had folded over onto themselves, underfoot, the insoles were too uncomfortable to walk on and so I had to go through the gaiter-and-shoe-removal routine every five minutes or so. That hadn't been much fun when I'd had a stone seat to sit on. Out here with nowhere to sit, hopping about in the driving rain with one shoe on and one shoe off, it was a significant nuisance.

Life got easier from Bloworth Crossing, though, because

---

[8] *Cup and ring carvings* are a common form of prehistoric art found in Atlantic Europe and Mediterranean Europe. They usually consist of a central concave depression, usually a few centimetres across, carved into a stone, surrounded by concentric rings, sometimes with a gutter leading out from the centre.

the path turned onto an old railway line, now a cinder track running along the top of the old railway embankment. The rain couldn't puddle or flood on the top of the embankment, and the cinder track was flat and even. Some of the water drained from my shoes and the insoles stopped sliding against the inside of the shoe.

Freed from the necessity to concentrate on my shoes, my mind was at liberty to think once more, despite the poor weather. Time to focus on positive thoughts, to get myself through the rain and the fog. I thought back to a piece of advice I'd been given before I set out on the Coast to Coast Walk.

"Savour every step; it will be over before you know it."

Oh, the wisdom contained in those eleven words! They came back to me again and again, especially (as now) in adversity, as I struggled towards the end of a long day with miles still to walk, as I forced myself up steep hills and as I squelched through bogs, as I struggled to keep dry in the rain and as I tried to avoid sunburn. What a metaphor for life! How often we concentrate on where we want to be instead of taking the time to enjoy life's journey. How little we comprehend the brevity of our existence and how often we fail to realise that our journey is far more important than our destination, which will in any case be the same for every one of us.

Savour every step; it will be over before you know it.

The wind parted the fog for a brief moment and, a little way ahead of me, I could see someone walking along the cinder track in the same direction as me. In front of him, pulling hard on his lead, I could just make out a small dog. Mike and Alfie!

I pushed on and soon caught them up. The route around the front of Kirby Bank had indeed been quicker than the ups and downs involved in crossing it. Mike held a single trekking pole in one hand and Alfie's lead in the other. He looked soaked and I guess I must have looked a bit bedraggled. Alfie, on the other hand, was still alert and inquisitive. I pointed this out to Mike.

"He doesn't seem to mind the weather, does he?"

Mike was well-used to his walking companion.

"We've been going for a hundred and fifty miles and he's still pulling on the lead."

We were both planning to stop at The Lion Inn, Blakey, so we agreed we'd meet there later and I pushed on ahead. After a few minutes I looked back through the rain, but they were already some way behind me, Alfie still enthusiastically straining at the leash.

If it had been a clear day I would have expected to see the inn from a long way off, but I realised that, cocooned in the shapeless, silent grey which surrounded me, it would be quite possible to walk past it without noticing. I checked my map again. Some way after the turning which led to the pub, the path I was on would cross a metalled road and I decided to use that as a catching feature. If I hit the road, I'd know that I must have gone past the pub.

To my left, a small footpath led off through the fog. It didn't look like the track I wanted but there was no path marked on my map at this point, so I walked up it to see if it led pubwards. The path took me around a small, stone-walled enclosure (also not on my map) and disappeared into the swirling fog. I paused and had a quick think. I could check this path a little further or I could go back to the main path and press on. If I went on up the small path and found the pub, my work was done. If I took the second option and missed the pub, I'd have to come back here and check the path. I decided to go on up the small path.

I crossed a patch of open moorland and spotted a wall on my right, leading away from me into the gloom. I'd been crossing open moor for miles, so I figured a wall must indicate at least some sort of human activity. I carried on and after a few more paces The Lion Inn materialised in front of my eyes. It was a big place and I was shocked that I had to be so close before I could see it, but that fact said more about the weather than it did about me.

Inside the pub, the barmaid was kindness personified. She told me in a strong Yorkshire accent that yes, of course I could camp, and then showed me the showers and the toilets, and a corridor with a heater where I could dry my clothes. I asked her where I should pitch my tent.

"As you came in, did you see wooden gate with a big *'no camping'* sign on it?"

"Yes."

"There."

I thanked her and made my way back outside, still in my wet things: I had to get the tent up before I started drying off and settling down. As I looked for a good site, I kept checking in the direction from which I'd approached the inn, but I couldn't see Mike and Alfie.

Even though I'd been told to, I didn't camp next to the gate with the *no camping* sign. The gate offered no shelter from the wind (which was whistling across the moor) and I felt that camping next to a sign telling me not to would have looked as if I was sticking up two fingers to the people who ran the pub (and who had been very nice to me). Instead, I found a flattish spot a little further on and set up in the lee of the wall I'd followed earlier.

Things were looking good: I had a sheltered camping spot, a way of drying out, and the prospect of cooked food, beer and an open fire for the evening. Wondering if Mike and Alfie had decided to miss out The Lion, I wandered back in to the bar. I hoped they'd make it because I felt I wouldn't mind some company for a change.

As if to emphasise that we don't always get what we want, I found I was the only customer in the bar. I ordered a drink and some nuts to take the edge off my hunger while I waited for the kitchen to commence operations, and made small talk with the barmaid. There must have been a 35 year age gap between us, in her favour, so the conversation didn't move much beyond perfunctory. I learned that, although she worked in a pub on the Coast to Coast Walk and met lots of Coast to Coast walkers, she had never walked it, had no desire to walk it, and thought people who did were mad. Since the thing had pretty much dominated my life for the last eleven days, there didn't seem much else to say.

I sat back and had a look around. The Lion is very proud of the fact that it's one of the oldest pubs in Yorkshire. The buildings date back to the 1500s, but it's quite probable that the presence of an inn on this site goes back several centuries before that. I felt very grateful to be in such a hospitable and welcoming place, the more so because it was in such an isolated spot. And then the door opened and a small but familiar dog entered, pulling hard on the lead attached to his collar, followed very quickly by Mike on the other end of the lead.

Mike checked that the pub was dog-friendly and then related to me how he'd walked straight past the pub in the fog and only realised it when he reached the road. The fog was so thick that even though Mike had walked to The Lion before, and even though he knew it was there, he'd still missed it. I realised that I'd probably found it more by luck than judgement and Mike's experience reinforced to both of us how careful we needed to be with our navigation up here in bad weather.

We spent a cosy and sociable evening tucked up in the snug of The Lion, by the fire. An evening notable for a significant discovery which I include here for the benefit of walkers everywhere: the discovery of the whiskey mattress. I found that the comfort afforded by my camping mat was increased exponentially by the consumption of several large ones before I slept on it. A useful tip for the backcountry, I decided, but you won't find it in *Scouting for Boys*.

I was up early the next morning and soon ready to go. The wind had dropped and the cloud seemed to have lifted, but when I got out of the tent I saw that the low-level stuff was still boiling and seething around the edges of the moor. As I struck camp, it rolled in slowly and inexorably, a horrible grey-green aerial sludge, blanking out everything as it advanced, like some ghastly First World War gas attack.

I was the only one up and about at this hour. Further down the field I could just about see what looked like a large, green bin liner with a hump in the middle of it. That was Mike's bivvy bag and the bulge was Alfie, sleeping on Mike's chest inside the bag. Next to them on the short grass was Mike's rucksack and next to that his single trekking pole, stuck into the ground but leaning over at an angle like an old marker post out on the moor. I silently wished them well and struck out for Priory Farm, 26km away.

I walked along a mix of small, metalled roads and gravel tracks so navigation wasn't too difficult even with the fog. I knew I had to stay up on the moor, follow a ridge along the north side of the valley of Glaisdale and then drop down into the village of the same name.

I made good time, notwithstanding the fog, and by the time I started the downhill stretch to Glaisdale, it had disappeared completely. It felt almost as if Nature were shrugging her shoulders: if I wasn't going to stay on the moor, then Nature wasn't going to play with me any more. I reached Glaisdale at 10am and felt slightly self-satisfied when I realised that the people who had stayed in bed and breakfast at The Lion would only have made a mile or two from the inn by this time.

I found a bench by the war memorial and made myself a hot drink. It was good to be off the moor and reaching civilisation emphasised how close I was to the end of my walk. I still found it difficult, I reflected, to regard Robin Hood's Bay as my destination, because it wasn't a place I wanted to get to. It wasn't the point of the walk. The *walk* was the point of the walk, but that's not a sentence which makes much sense on a first reading. Or a second.

Maybe Robert Louis Stevenson had it right when he said, "To travel hopefully is a better thing than to arrive." Or maybe Stevenson over-egged it, maybe simply *to travel* is a better thing than to arrive. So much depends upon your experiences while travelling and on what is waiting for you at your destination. In my case, with only the sea waiting for me at journey's end and a cracking walk almost in the bag, the journey was most definitely the thing.

My map seemed to indicate nothing more than a stroll through hilly farmland and downwards to the coast for the next day and a half, but I'd underestimated the genius of the man who devised this walk.

From Glaisdale my path followed the swirling, gravy-brown River Esk through East Arncliff Wood. The green, closed-in woodland felt surprisingly comforting after the bleak exposure of the moors.

The next village was Egton Bridge and I decided to stop for lunch at the pub there. It was a good decision: no sooner was I through the pub door than the heavens opened. I looked out of the bar's window and watched the rain bouncing back up, off the street outside.

"Just in time," remarked the barman, as if admiring some particularly shrewd judgement on my part.

I found myself a table, a task made easy by virtue of the fact that I was the only customer, and ordered some food. I hoped they wouldn't be too quick in bringing it – I didn't have far to walk from Egton Bridge but I hoped to do it dry.

I was joined at my table by three elderly men, all obviously friends of very long-standing. I was still the only other customer in the pub but they made a beeline for my table and sat themselves around it. The table was easily big enough for eight people, but they all managed to seat themselves at my end of it. They were obviously "locals" and I knew that I might be sitting at their usual table, so I offered to move and let them have the whole thing, but they'd have none of it. That flash of consideration was the nearest they came to hospitality. More significantly, I found, it also meant that I was unable to escape their conversation and that turned out to be truly dire.

They started with a detailed analysis of everything that was wrong with a recent race meeting. Horses, jockeys, stables, trainers and owners were all dissected at great length by individuals who knew better and weren't shy about saying so. Each man spoke with a sort of weighty gravitas, as if his every sentence was of profound importance, and they delighted in filling in the holes in each other's knowledge. They appeared to have known every racehorse-owner, every jockey and every groom since boyhood, and I quickly came to realise that each of them saw himself as an expert on pretty much every subject. I was reminded of something I'd been told a long time ago:

"You can always tell a Yorkshireman. But you can't tell him much."

I wondered how the landlord put up with this nonsense on a daily basis and that thought made me wonder about the suicide rate amongst pub licensees in these parts.

Their subject changed and became that of a mutual acquaintance, a man known to all of them, who apparently combined a taste for expensive cars with a shocking inability to drive them. They started working through a catalogue of vehicles by model and date, and bickered and corrected each other as they listed the accident which had destroyed each of them, with precise locations and details of any witnesses. Whenever one of them got up for any reason, they simply carried on the conversation and they often talked straight across me as if I wasn't there, or talked over my head to involve the licensee and, less often, the barman.

By this stage, I'd given up on the suicide statistics for pub landlords and was speculating about the figures for murders committed by Coast to Coast hikers. I felt like telling them to pack it in, that I didn't give a tinker's cuss whether Mary was in the Range Rover when it hit the wall or in the Jag when it went into the river and that if they had any sort of life worth living, neither would they. But I felt as if I was in *their* pub, and to an extent I suppose I was. I realised, with a start, that I was bolting my food, and that the downpour outside, together with the prospect of a total drenching, didn't seem quite as bad as I'd first thought.

From the hallway outside the bar, I heard the door from the street open and close and then that sound that people make when they step from heavy rain into a nice dry building. Then waterproofs being taken off and shaken and, finally, Rob came in.

I'd last seen him in a coffee shop in Richmond, if you remember. I usually get along fine with just my own company on a long walk, but I was never so glad to see a familiar face as I was in that pub in Egton Bridge. The conversational one-upmanship around me had turned to the subject of allotments, but it no longer mattered, I was free.

I'd finished my meal and Rob was halfway through his when, out in the hallway, the street door opened and closed, and again there was the sound of waterproofs being taken off and shaken. Before the shaking had quite finished, the door into the bar burst open and Alfie the dog hurtled in, brought to an abrupt, almost neck-breaking halt by the lead which was still attached to his collar and to which he appeared completely and good-naturedly indifferent. He was closely followed by Mike.

Rob left, back out into the rain to resume his hike, but I stayed for another pint with Mike and Alfie, pleased to see them again. Mike had a bed and breakfast booked in Grosmont, a village about 1km after the site where I was planning to camp, so we arranged to meet in the pub there later that evening.

I pressed on, out of Egton Bridge, leaving behind me a spirited debate about angling, being deliberated by men who knew all there was to know on the subject, and headed for Grosmont. I was on the last strip of my strip map and that fact alone gave me a lift. Whenever I opened my map to the relevant fold, there was I on one edge of it and there was the sea on the other edge. My walk was almost in the bag!

I walked along a permissive path between the river and the steam railway line but if any steam trains were running, I couldn't see or hear them. The walk to Priory Farm was an easy stroll along an old toll road, into some trees where a lane crossed a stream, turn left onto the lane and there was the farm. The camping field, directly in front of the farmhouse, didn't have many flat spaces, but I managed to find one big enough for my tent and to put the tent up just before the rain came in again. I retired to the helpfully signed *Campers' Kitchen and WC* to consider my next move.

I watched the rain on the window while my phone charged and my coffee cooled. By the time I was finished the rain had stopped, so I wandered back to the field and checked my tent. I'd left it properly pitched only an hour ago, but now it looked as if it had been put up by a drunk who didn't care because he wasn't going to sleep in it.

One of the problems with tents made from nylon is that the fabric sags when the tent gets wet. Slack fabric makes a noise in the night as it blows about and, as it moves, it flicks condensation down onto you and your sleeping bag inside the tent. Unless you keep getting up in the night and repeatedly re-tension the tent, or you only go walking in a dry climate, nylon is always going to sag. This particular tent had been with me through thick and thin, and had never let me down, so I had a soft spot for it, but after this trip I moved on to cuben fibre and I've never looked back. Cuben is waterproof, doesn't sag, and, get this, a similar sized tent in cuben fibre weighs about a third of the weight of a nylon one. A third! It's cuben all the way for me.

I re-tensioned Old Faithful, gathered up my few valuables (my camera, phone, front door key, etc.) and started the mile-or-so walk to The Station Tavern, where Mike and Alfie were rooming.

I'd defy anyone to walk up the main street in Grosmont and not feel as if they had been transported back to the 1930s. The big railway yard full of steam locomotives and the station platforms lined with the old brown and cream carriages contribute much of this ambience, but they're only part of the story. The individual houses and shops all look as if their owners liked the 30s and simply decided to stay there. I found it a little unnerving at first, and then relaxing and comforting. By the time I got to the pub, I was wondering why the rest of us were living in the twenty-first century, and whether we even realise that we have a choice. The pub brought me back to earth, though. Grosmont's commitment to times past didn't extent to the price of its beer – there was nothing 1930s about that.

Mike and Alfie came down to the bar and we talked over the day's walking, as walkers do. Two other men joined us, Coast to Coast hikers who were also rooming at The Station Tavern, and we discussed the Wainwright walk. One of them expressed his admiration for what he called, "You blokes who do it all in one hit," and I found that they were walking the Coast to Coast a little at a time and that they had completed about half of it so far. I asked how long they'd been doing this. The reply surprised me.

"Four years."

Four years and only halfway? I couldn't believe I'd heard correctly and I had to check. My fellow hiker confirmed what he'd just told me: half of it done in four years.

I told him I couldn't escape the impression that his heart wasn't really in it, and then regretted what I'd said because he looked hurt by it. Maybe I'd got the wrong end of the stick, I thought, maybe this walk really is too good to rush and maybe you should draw it out and savour it. But, eight years to complete a two-week walk? Come on! There's drawing it out and savouring it, and then there's sheer, bone-idle laziness.

The subject changed to camping and they asked me if I was camping to save money. That made me stop and think for a second, because I'd never thought of camping as a cheaper option. I pointed that out first.

"If you knew how much some of my kit cost, you might not think camping was a money-saver."

I prefer camping, I went on, because of the freedom it gives me. I felt almost lyrical about the subject and so I indulged myself and let it flow a little. I tend to wake when the sun comes up, so even after a lie-in and a leisurely breakfast, I'm usually back on the trail by 6 o'clock each morning in the summer. By the time the people in bed and breakfast start walking, I've got eight or nine miles under my belt, at what is often the most beautiful time of the day. I always have my accommodation with me, so if the weather gets ugly I can, if I want, chuck the tent up and have an early night wherever I happen to find myself. Or, if I reach my planned destination earlier than I'd intended, I have the option to press on if I want to, secure in the knowledge that I'll have no accommodation worries when I eventually decide to stop. I keep myself clean and warm, and I don't carry much in the way of kit, in fact my rucksack is lighter than most walkers' day sacks.

Over to you. Sell me bed and breakfast.

However, other than a general feeling that hot showers and soft beds were essential to support life and the thought that a cooked breakfast was "nice", they didn't have much to offer. They certainly didn't communicate anything like passion for their walking or for their choice of accommodation. I finished the evening wondering why they bothered. To each, his own, I suppose.

I was lucky enough to have a dry walk back to the tent, although there were several heavy rain showers later in the night. It was still thrashing it down at 5.30am, when I decided it was time to make a start.

Before I got up, I lay in my sleeping bag for a few minutes and thought the thing through.

Today would be my last day, my last chance to enjoy this walk. I had 27km to walk to get to Robin Hood's Bay (that's about 17 miles in old money). I'd walk through valleys and forests, and over moorland and through bogs. Then, at last, I'd reach the sea again, this time on the other side of England. I couldn't wait to get started and I had to temper my enthusiasm, to make myself slow down and think it through. If I got up now, struck camp and charged off, I'd get soaked and so would most of my kit. And there would still be the question of breakfast.

I decided I would carefully pack up everything that had to be kept dry, while I was still inside the tent. There wasn't much of that: my sleeping bag, gloves, woolly hat, spare socks and so on. I'd stow that lot in my rucksack, add the other stuff so that it was all in one place and easily carried, and then step outside in my waterproofs. I'd dismantle the tent as quickly as I could, grab up everything and hightail it for the *Campers' Kitchen and WC*. Safely ensconced in the dry, I'd get breakfast and repack my kit so that my walking bits and pieces were on top of my camping things, and thus readily on hand throughout the day.

The plan worked well and soon I was striding along Eskdaleside, Grosmont's main street, the clacking of my trekking poles the only sound so early in the morning. The rain was fading as I passed The Station Tavern, with Mike and Alfie still asleep inside, and started up the steep hill leading out of town, eager to get the miles done.

When I reached the top, there was no escaping the feeling that I was back on the moors again. Brown, scrubby heather stretched away from me in every direction and solid grey clouds topped things off overhead. Unlike the last few days, the clouds were higher and so didn't hinder my navigation. They were even high enough off the ground for me to fancy I saw the few of High Bride Stones which are still standing, over to my right as I crossed Sleight Moor.

The sun was struggling to come out as I reached the "A" road and found the path that would take me down to Littlebeck, and I remembered that the forecast was for full sun from 2pm. I'd been up here for long enough to know that, weatherwise, I needed to be ready for anything at any time, so I didn't set much store by the forecast.

Littlebeck is a pretty little village and it didn't take long for me to find the muddy track which would take me through the woods alongside May Beck.

I passed the old cave that is the last remnant of alum extraction near Littlebeck and paused to peer into it. I couldn't see how deep it went and the loose, shaley rock deterred me from stepping in. The whole thing looked as if it could give way at any moment.

Alum was used in the dying of cloth and its extraction proved a profitable business here through the 1600s and 1700s. The alum industry is now long-gone from Little Beck Wood and if you didn't know it had been here, you'd be unlikely to notice any sign of it.

Dark and unknown under the silver birches, the cave had a strange, other-worldly feel to it. I moved on up the path and came to The Hermitage.

The Hermitage was carved many years ago from the bedrock protruding from the slope ahead of me, and surrounded by leaf mould and beech trees. A door has been carved into the front of it and if you walk inside you'll find a bench seat and floor, all hewn from the living rock. Over the front door is the legend:

The locals have it that The Hermitage was created as a folly by an unemployed seamen, on the instructions of George Chubb, a local schoolmaster, possibly as an employment scheme. On top of it are two stone chairs: sit in one to make a wish and then in the other to ensure your wish comes true.

I love places like this and I loafed about inside The Hermitage until I started to get cold and then went outside and hung around a bit more. I debated whether to make myself a hot drink but decided against it. There was nowhere to sit comfortably outside The Hermitage and I didn't want to fire up my stove inside it. And there was supposed to be a tearoom just a little further along the trail, so I took a few more photographs and went back to picking my way through the beech trees.

The path along the beck through Great Wood was a delight, woodland walking at its best, and I reached Falling Foss in good spirits. Falling Foss is a 10m waterfall in a deep woodland setting. It looked stunning and I was pleased to see the tearoom right next to it as I approached. When I got there, I was marginally less chuffed to see that the tearoom was firmly closed. Undaunted, I threw off my rucksack, grabbed one of the picnic tables and made myself a mug of hot chocolate while I enjoyed the view and the roar of water on rock. Then I made myself another and ate a whole bag of sweets, all to lighten my pack, you understand. I started packing away and was just about to leave when a teenage girl arrived and opened up the teashop. She was out by about ten minutes, because by that stage I'd reached my capacity for sugar consumption.

I followed the path out of the wood and onto Sheaton Low Moor. I knew this moor was small and should be easy going, and so it proved until I got about two thirds of the way across it.

The narrow, dry, bare-earth footpath gave way to grass, and the grass gave way to grass under a couple of inches of clear water. It wasn't long before the water got deeper and darker, and soon I was sloshing along in it, ankle-deep.

I paused to work out the best route through. I seemed to have been in water for quite some time and there weren't any obvious dry bits. I was already in up to my ankles but I could see the stile I wanted a hundred metres or so away. Since my feet were already wet, I found myself tempted to crash on in a straight line as quickly as I could.

But something, some indefinable impulse, made me pause and probe the bog ahead of me with my trekking pole. I'm not sure why I did it; I'd crossed plenty of bogs in the preceding 250km and I'd never felt the need to test the depth of any of them, but I did this time.

As I leaned forward and pushed my pole in, the bog swallowed it right to the handle with no bottom. If I'd continued straight ahead, within two paces I would have been up to my chest in cold, murky water, maybe even deeper.

I gulped and tried the bog to my left and then to my right: the same in each case.

I realised that I was standing in the middle of a bog, on a small promontory. The top of the promontory was about nine inches below the surface of the water and my soundings told me that it sloped away steeply on three sides. I retraced my steps very carefully. As I did so I contemplated what it might have felt like to fall unexpectedly into deep, slimy water. Would I have been able to unfasten and shrug off my rucksack before it dragged me under? If I was able to ditch it, how would I retrieve it again from the depths of the bog? And how would I cope in the next village with my phone, money and credit cards all ruined by water and dirt? What would I do if I lost my shoes?

I put all that out of my head and picked my way carefully out of the bog, cautiously probing ahead of me with a walking pole like a soldier feeling his way out of a minefield with a bayonet. I got to the other side without going more than knee-deep and it felt like a major achievement in the circumstances. I looked back the way I'd just come. The bog looked deceptively innocent, but I knew it for the worst I'd encountered in nearly two hundred miles.

I carried on down the lane ahead of me. The sun was coming out and I'd escaped the bog. I felt pretty good. And then, without warning, the bog took its revenge: the still-wet insoles in my shoes slid forwards and scrunched up under my feet, both feet almost simultaneously.

I swore. Then I stopped walking and removed my gaiters and my shoes, and straightened out the insoles. I made about five paces before the same thing happened again.

The shoes were clearly unwearable in their current state and I had about 11km still to walk. I went through the gaiter/shoe removal ritual again but this time I put the shoes back on without the insoles. I had to really work the shoelaces because, without the insoles in them, my shoes were much too big for my feet. I was convinced I could do it. After all, 11km is only three hours' walking. The insoles I placed in a net pocket on the outside of my pack in an effort to dry them[9].

Without insoles, my shoes were not as uncomfortable as I'd anticipated they would be. They felt different and I had to re-lace them a few times before I got it right, but they didn't chafe.

I stopped at The Hare and Hounds in the village of Hawkser for a swift pint and sat outside chatting with a couple who were day-walking.

"As you leave Hawkser," they told me, "Turn onto a cinder track to walk into Robin Hood's Bay. It's higher up than the path along the cliffs and the views are better."

They showed me on my map and I decided I'd take their advice. It was, after all, entirely in keeping with the spirit of Wainwright's walk to forge my own route.

I thanked my new friends and moved off from the bench outside the pub just as the drizzle began. A few minutes later I could see the sea! My walk was almost over and I felt a great

---

[9] When I got home, I wrote to the makers to ask why they didn't use insoles which would retain their rigidity in the wet. I received a rather sniffy reply telling me that the shoes were designed for running, not walking (as if runners never go outside in the rain!)

rush of elation that I'd almost walked from one coast, clean across the country to the other.

I soon found the cinder track and started down it – it was an old railway line and I could see the advice had been good, particularly for someone whose shoes were folded-over and roped up tight because they were too big. By the time I was a hundred metres down the track, the weather gave up any pretensions it might have had and the heavens opened. I didn't care a jot: I could see the sea and it was all I could think about.

Chapter 6

The Finish

The North Sea, on failing to meet the dress code, smuggling, criminal wrecking, Victorian recycling and the proper order of things.

There were any number of approaches I could have taken to Robin Hood's Bay. I could have followed the road into town, or any of the footpaths close to the road. I could have stuck with Wainwright's preferred entry route, along the clifftops following the coast line. I took the old railway line for the views and sure enough it gave me good views, even in the rain. I kept stopping and staring, mesmerised by the sea I'd walked so long to get to.

The North Sea was grey, flat and calm, and being rained on. In the far distance, it seemed to rise up to meet the grey sky at a darker band on the horizon, where the sky appeared to curve down to meet it. I could just discern the silhouettes of ships far out to sea. The sea and the sky combined to produce a symphony of drab greyness, but my walk to get there made this view more beautiful than the Amalfi coast. I felt as if I could actually inhale the view.

I set off for Robin Hood's Bay with some reluctance, because it would mean the end of my journey.

I was passing more and more people as I got closer to the village. It was tipping with rain and I was well-wrapped up in waterproof jacket and overtrousers, but I was definitely an oddity as I walked along the cinder track. Everyone else was dressed as if for an afternoon on a Mediterranean beach, in shorts, vests and flip flops. In what I could only determine to be either self-delusion or reckless optimism, every second person seemed to be wearing sunglasses. Families and couples, they were, without exception, soaked to the skin by the rain. When I paused to look out at the sea I felt chilly despite my layers of clothing, so they must have been cold. But, in a strange inversion of the natural order of things, they looked at me as if I was mad. The result was a cumulative one and by the time I reached the edge of Robin Hood's Bay, I'd developed a strong and slightly uncomfortable feeling that this place had a dress code and that I was failing to meet it.

Robin Hood's Bay, or "Bay Town" as the locals call it, is set in a cleft in the cliffs which allows access to the sea. The oldest houses and the steepest streets and alleyways are all jumbled higgledy-piggledy into this crack in the ground. The place gradually spread up the hill and back onto the clifftop, and by the time the railway came in 1885 the site of the station was probably also the edge of the town.

The station was closed in 1965 and it's now holiday accommodation, a change that reflects the fortunes of the town, which is now very definitely a holiday destination. But, even packed to the gills with trippers, Robin Hood's Bay still manages to retain its old-world charm.

I arrived at the site of the old railway station and that point marked the end of level walking for me. From then on I went down a street that sloped like the chute of a children's slide, with old houses and tiny ginnels crowding in from each side. I'd read somewhere that many of the houses are linked by old smuggling tunnels. It didn't seem likely, because tunnelling would have been an awful lot of work in a place like this, but who knows? Maybe the smuggling was profitable enough to make it worthwhile.

And make no mistake: smuggling was very profitable. The town plays up its smuggling history for the benefit of the tourists, but it's true that smuggling was big business here. In some ways it would have been strange if this had not been the case: spirits, tobacco and tea were all smuggled extensively along this coast in the eighteenth century. In Robin Hood's Bay in 1773, the smugglers felt sure enough of themselves to take on two excise cutters, and the revenue men were outgunned and driven out of the bay by the smuggler vessels. In 1779, smugglers fought a pitched battle with the revenue men on the Bay Town dockside, to retain control of a cargo of brandy, gin, and tea. I wondered if George Chubb, the schoolmaster who'd paid for The Hermitage at Littlebeck, used to drink contraband brandy.

Smuggling was a result of the punitive taxes levied by the government to pay for a century of expensive European wars. The tax on tea, for instance, was almost 70% of its initial cost. Pushing up the prices of so many goods by imposing high taxes created a significant business opportunity for those who could import and sell their goods tax-free, albeit illegally. While the extent and the cost of these taxes had risen considerably, the government's method of collecting them had not developed much since the thirteenth century and centred on a series of customs houses at coastal ports. With most goods highly taxed and in great demand, and an inefficient system of tax collection and law enforcement, the circumstances were ripe for the "free-traders".

Smuggling stayed profitable for a long time. It wasn't until the 1840s that Britain adopted a free trade policy which significantly reduced import duties and, in consequence, killed off smuggling.

Of course, Bay Town's connection with the sea long pre-dates the smuggling era and carries on to this day. Just a few years ago, when a house here was being refurbished, two large timber joists were discovered. One had the word *Ipswich* carved into it, and the other the words *Elizabeth Jan.*

The timbers came from a brig called *Elizabeth Jane.* Built at Guysborough in Nova Scotia, Canada, in 1817, by 1830 the *Elizabeth Jane* had been sold on and was registered at Ipswich. From 1846 she was owned by a Mr William Read.

Just two years before, Read had been tried at the Central Criminal Court in London[10], charged alongside one of his captains with deliberately sinking a ship in order to claim the insurance money. Read was acquitted of that charge, but the captain was convicted and sentenced to be transported for life.

By 1854, *Elizabeth Jane* was in a poor state and she spent the first few months of that year on the rocks near Newbiggin-by-the-Sea in the north-east of England. Her owners got her back to Ipswich, although in a leaky state, and in July she was sent to collect a cargo of coal from Sunderland. On the return voyage, she sprang a leak off Whitby and her crew abandoned her near Robin Hood's Bay, where she went aground.

After that, it seems that Mr Moses Bell, a local opportunist, salvaged timber from the wreck and was able to use it to add a further two storeys to his house in Robin Hood's Bay. There the beams sat, undisturbed until renovation started in 2003.

Whether or not William Read arranged the abandonment and, ultimately, the wrecking of *Elizabeth Jane* is, of course, a matter for conjecture.

The rain was easing as I made my way down steep New Road to get to the sea. I paused at The Bay Hotel and noted the plaque on its wall, telling me that it marked the end of the Coast to Coast Walk. It doesn't, of course. The walk ends when I say it ends.

With that in mind, I decided it was time to complete my walk and I turned to the slipway which leads down to the sea. If the tide had been out, I'd have had to walk about a mile across the beach, out over sand and rocks, in order to dip my foot and complete my walk. As if to recompense me for my long walk to the sea at St Bees, at Robin Hood's Bay the tide was in and lapping at the slipway. It seemed only fair and I felt a strong sense of natural balance, of eternal equilibrium and the proper

---

[10]   The *Central Criminal Court* is better known as *the Old Bailey,* after the street in which it stands.

order of things as I walked down the slip and dipped my shoe in the North Sea.

I walked back up the slipway, through the crowds of holiday-makers who had flooded back out of the cafés and shops now that the rain had stopped. An old fellow saw my rucksack and stopped to talk with me.

"You just done the Coast to Coast?"

I nodded, "Yes."

He pointed up some steps. "You want to get in there and get a certificate to prove you've done it. Only a few quid."

I laughed. "I don't need a certificate."

He looked aghast, as if I'd said something appalling or confessed to something inexcusable.

"But no-one will believe you've done it if you don't get a certificate."

I was uncharacteristically blunt.

"I don't care what they believe. I know I've done it. Boy, do I know I've done it."

I turned and walked back up the hill.

Part 2

Chapter 7

Using Part 2

The second part of this book aims to help walkers prepare for and hike the Coast to Coast Walk. While the majority of the information is specific to this hike, some of it might seem generic to long-distance walking, however a glance at other walkers on the CtoC will quickly show why it needs to be re-stated.

Like any long walk, the Coast to Coast Walk is only a series of short walks stuck together. But it needs a "long walk" mentality because, as one hiker said to me, "It messes with your head, if you let it." And that's the point: if you let it. Shakespeare summed it up perfectly when he said, "There's nothing good or bad, but thinking makes it so." You can't control the hills, the wind, the rain or the sunshine, but you can control your own thinking, your attitude towards this walk.

Good planning will increase the likelihood of a successful completion, and accurate information is essential in order to plan. Chapter 8 contains a route assessment which details what a Coast to Coast walker can expect in terms of weather and climate (both average and extreme), terrain, hazards, etc. Chapter 9 contains route data: details of distances, towns, villages, and facilities of interest to walkers, all along the route. Chapter 10 contains more general information for anyone planning their hike, covering subjects such as accommodation, equipment, preparation and so on.

One of the first decisions any walker must make is, in which direction to walk?

Most walkers do as Wainwright did and start at the west coast, then walk eastwards. This has the advantage that the prevailing wind is at your back and it ensures that the steepest parts of the walk, in the Lake District, are completed early on. Since west-to-east is the most popular way to complete the Coast to Coast Walk, it's also the way outlined in this book.

Some walkers do hike east-to-west and this has the advantage that what is arguably the most scenic part of the walk, the Lake District, is saved until the end. Since most people walk west-to-east, anyone walking east-to-west will meet lots of hikers travelling in the more traditional direction (but, in most cases, will meet them only once!)

Either direction is equally valid, of course, as long as you enjoy it.

Walkers also need to decide the route they will take.

The Coast to Coast Walk isn't marked on Ordnance Survey (OS) maps since, a) it isn't a national trail, and, b) its architect, Alfred Wainwright, deliberately chose not to set a definitive route. That said, most guidebooks and non-OS maps show almost identical routes, with variations according to the time of year so as to minimise footpath and environmental erosion. Ultimately, however, it's up to each hiker to decide the route they'd like to walk.

A note about units used in Part 2 of this book:

At the time of writing, every country in the world has adopted the metric system except those giants of individual liberty: the USA, Burma and Liberia. That means that in most areas of life the UK now uses the metric system. This is a sensible change which started back in the year dot, but which will probably never be brought to full completion because the metric system was invented by the French. This lack of closure results in a situation where people buy pints of beer but litres of petrol, and talk about distance in miles but carpet in square metres.

As far as hiking is concerned, the country's national mapping (the Ordnance Survey) is entirely metric. Throughout Part 2 distances are given in kilometres because a grid square on most maps measures 1km by 1km on the ground, and thus it's very easy to estimate distance in kilometres using the grid squares. Because not everyone is comfortable with metric units, US/Imperial measures are included where practicable.

Chapter 8

Route Assessment

An accurate and detailed assessment of your proposed hike is important because, with the route data contained in the following chapter, it will inform your decisions on equipment, skills, clothing and food.

Weather details are given for each month of the year using measurements taken at the Warcop Range weather station. Warcop Range is near the halfway point of the Coast to Coast, at an altitude of 227m (745ft). The average figures for each month give a good idea of what can expected during that month, while the record highs and lows give an idea of what the weather is capable of in this part of the world.

The hours of daylight available, considered with the information on terrain and vegetation, should allow at least a rough calculation of probable daily mileage, and thus of food and accommodation requirements.

Issues arising from remoteness and natural hazards will be particularly useful for those planning to hike alone - a perfectly reasonable proposition and more on that later.

Route Assessment: The Coast to Coast Walk

Distance / Height
Distance: 309km / 192mi
Ascent: 8,550m / 28,051ft
Highest point: Kidsty Pike, 780m / 2,560ft
Lowest point: Sea level (St Bees and Robin Hood's Bay).
                   Inland: Danby Wiske, 35m / 115ft.

Climate and Weather

January
Temperature, average high: 6C / 43°F
Temperature, average low: 1C / 35°F
Temperature, record high: 15C / 59°F
Temperature, record low: -9C / 16°F
Precipitation, total: 88mm / 3.5in
Precipitation type / frequency: rain, snow / 15 days
Humidity: 85%
Wind, average: 19km/h / 12mph
Wind, record: 91km/h / 56mph
Sunshine: 3hrs/day
Sunrise / sunset: 0819 / 1618
Daylight: 7h 59m

February
Temperature, average high: 6C / 44°F
Temperature, average low: 1C / 34°F
Temperature, record high: 14C / 57°F
Temperature, record low: -9C / 16°F
Precipitation, total: 70mm / 3in
Precipitation type / frequency: rain, snow / 12 days
Humidity: 84%
Wind, average: 19km/h / 12mph
Wind, record: 94km/h / 59mph
Sunshine: 4hrs/day
Sunrise / sunset: 0727 / 1719

Daylight:	9h 52m

March

Temperature, average high:	8C / 47°F
Temperature, average low:	2C / 36°F
Temperature, record high:	20C / 68°F
Temperature, record low:	-9C / 16°F
Precipitation, total:	52mm / 2in
Precipitation type / frequency:	rain, snow / 13 days
Humidity:	80%
Wind, average:	19km/h / 12mph
Wind, record:	81km/h / 51mph
Sunshine:	5hrs/day
Sunrise / sunset:	0621 / 1815
Daylight:	11h 54m

April

Temperature, average high:	11C / 51°F
Temperature, average low:	3C / 38°F
Temperature, record high:	23C / 74°F
Temperature, record low:	-6C / 21°F
Precipitation, total:	45mm / 2in
Precipitation type / frequency:	rain / 11 days
Humidity:	76%
Wind, average:	18km/h / 11mph
Wind, record:	83km/h / 52mph
Sunshine:	7hrs/day
Sunrise / sunset:	0604 / 2014
Daylight:	14h 10m

May

Temperature, average high:	14C / 58°F
Temperature, average low:	6C / 43°F
Temperature, record high:	26C / 78°F
Temperature, record low:	-2C / 28°F
Precipitation, total:	45mm / 2in
Precipitation type / frequency:	rain / 11 days

Humidity:	74%
Wind, average:	17km/h / 11mph
Wind, record:	87km/h / 54mph
Sunshine:	7hrs/day
Sunrise / sunset:	0500 / 2112
Daylight:	16h 12m

June

Temperature, average high:	17C / 62°F
Temperature, average low:	8C / 47°F
Temperature, record high:	28C / 82°F
Temperature, record low:	-11C / 12°F
Precipitation, total:	48mm / 2in
Precipitation type / frequency:	rain / 11 days
Humidity:	77%
Wind, average:	14km/h / 9mph
Wind, record:	80km/h / 49mph
Sunshine:	8hrs/day
Sunrise / sunset:	0430 / 2149
Daylight:	17h 19m

July

Temperature, average high:	19C / 66°F
Temperature, average low:	11C / 52°F
Temperature, record high:	30C / 86°F
Temperature, record low:	3C / 38°F
Precipitation, total:	52mm / 2in
Precipitation type / frequency:	rain / 11 days
Humidity:	78%
Wind, average:	13km/h / 8mph
Wind, record:	122km/h / 76mph
Sunshine:	7hrs/day
Sunrise / sunset:	0452 / 2139
Daylight:	16h 47m

August

Temperature, average high:	18C / 65°F

Temperature, average low:	10C / 51°F
Temperature, record high:	30C / 86°F
Temperature, record low:	-18C / -1°F
Precipitation total:	62mm / 2.5in
Precipitation type / frequency:	rain / 12 days
Humidity:	79%
Wind, average:	13km/h / 8mph
Wind, record:	70km/h / 44mph
Sunshine:	5hrs/day
Sunrise / sunset:	0544 / 2043
Daylight:	14h 59m

September

Temperature, average high:	16C / 60°F
Temperature, average low:	8C / 47°F
Temperature, record high:	25C / 77°F
Temperature, record low:	-1C / 29°F
Precipitation, total:	64mm / 2.5in
Precipitation type / frequency:	rain / 11 days
Humidity:	81%
Wind, average:	15km/h / 9mph
Wind, record:	80km/h / 49mph
Sunshine:	5hrs/day
Sunrise / sunset:	0641 / 1927
Daylight:	12h 46m

October

Temperature, average high:	12C / 54°F
Temperature, average low:	6C / 43°F
Temperature, record high:	21C / 70°F
Temperature, record low:	-6C / 21°F
Precipitation, total:	85mm / 3.5in
Precipitation type / frequency:	rain / 16 days
Humidity:	83%
Wind, average:	16km/h / 10mph
Wind, record:	83km/h / 52mph
Sunshine:	5hrs/day

Sunrise / sunset:	0737 / 1813
Daylight:	10h 36m

November

Temperature, average high:	8C / 47°F
Temperature, average low:	3C / 38°F
Temperature, record high:	16C / 60°F
Temperature record low:	-10C / 14°F
Precipitation, total:	75mm / 3in
Precipitation type / frequency:	rain, snow / 15 days
Humidity:	85%
Wind, average:	16km/h / 10mph
Wind, record:	78km/h / 48mph
Sunshine:	3hrs/day
Sunrise / sunset:	0738 / 1610
Daylight:	8h 32m

December

Temperature, average high:	6C / 43°F
Temperature, average low:	1C / 34°F
Temperature, record high:	14C / 56°F
Temperature, record low:	-11C / 13°F
Precipitation, total:	86mm / 3.5in
Precipitation type / frequency:	rain, snow / 14 days
Humidity:	86%
Wind, average:	17km/h / 10mph
Wind, record:	96km/h / 60mph
Sunshine:	3hrs/day
Sunrise / sunset:	0823 / 1546
Daylight:	7h 23m

Terrain

Footpaths and farm tracks, along coastal paths, through farmland, valleys, over mountains, bogs, moorland. Mud, rocks, uneven ground.

Vegetation

Mostly mountain and moorland. Some farmland, some deciduous forest, some coniferous forest.

Vegetation density is low.

The main allergens are pollens. Their peak release periods are:

Grass pollen:	June and July.
Tree pollen:	mid-February to mid-July.
Weed pollen:	May to mid-August.

Navigational Aids

The route is mostly open in aspect, although visibility will depend on the weather conditions.

Identifiable hills and lakes in the Lake District assist navigation.

The route follows existing paths and tracks. Some "footpath" signs are in evidence but Coast to Coast signs are rare.

Sun Exposure

The altitude of this walk varies between sea level and 780m. There is very little natural sun protection.

Availability of Water and Food

Water is readily available from campsites, pubs, bed and breakfast establishments, public conveniences, shops (bottled water) and from upland streams. Avoid streams in areas grazed by livestock and treat stream water before drinking.

Food is not difficult to obtain, whether from pubs, cafes and restaurants or from shops. The data sheet shows the main sources of food. If you intend to depend on local shops, check their opening hours in advance.

Problematic Wildlife

Farm dogs – risk of bite.
Ticks – risk of Lyme's Disease.
The likelihood of either is very low.

Remoteness

The remotest stretches of the Coast to Coast Walk are:

Ennerdale, Rosthwaite to Grasmere (12km),

Grasmere to Patterdale (12km),

Patterdale to Shap (24km),

Kirkby Stephen to Keld (18km),

Keld to Reeth (17km),

Catterick Bridge to Ingleby Cross (27km),

Ingleby Cross to The Lion Inn, Blakey (33km).

In the event of an emergency, possible barriers to self-rescue include steep slopes and rough terrain, both coinciding with areas of poor mobile phone reception.

Natural Hazards

Heavy rain (risk of wet kit, wet clothing and exposure).

Fog (can adversely affect navigation).

Deep and extensive bogs.

Steep, uneven slopes.

Combinations of the above.

Chapter 9

Route Data

In this chapter, the route of the Coast to Coast Walk is described from west to east. When walking, find your location on the path and then refer to the data sheet. By that method you will be able to plan ahead in order to re-provision, visit interesting sites, camp, etc.

For each location, distances are shown in bold. Distance is shown from the last location and cumulatively from the start of the walk (in brackets), in both kilometres and miles. The location name is shown in italics, followed by its facilities, then places of interest, thus:

Km from last (cum km) / Miles from last (cum miles)
Place name
Facilities.
Places of interest.

Indented entries are off the trail.

Shops, pubs, post offices, etc., sometimes change their opening hours and the services they offer, so if you intend to depend heavily upon one or more facilities, check before you leave!

The following abbreviations are used:

ATM: automatic teller machine (cash machine).
B&B: bed and breakfast establishment.
PH: public house (pub).
PO: Post Office.
WC: public toilet (often with drinking water available).
YHA: Youth Hostel Association (although no age limit).
An "off licence" is a shop licensed to sell intoxicating liquor for consumption off the premises only.

Route Data: The Coast to Coast Walk

0.0km (0.0km cumulative) / 0mi (0mi cumulative)
St Bees
Camping (Seacote Park, Beach Road), PH, WC, shops, PO.

5km (5km) / 3.1mi (3.1mi)
St Bees Lighthouse.

> 6km / 3.7mi
> (and 1km off route)
> *Tarnflat Hall.*
> Camping barn.

8.0km (8.0km) / 5mi (5mi)
Sandwith
PH.

5.2km (13.2km) / 3.25mi (8.25mi)
Moor Row

1.6km (14.8km) / 1mi (9.25mi)
Cleator
Family store / off licence, hotel, PH.

8.4km (23.2km) / 5.25mi (14.5mi)
Low Cock How
Camping (Low Cock How Farm) 2km before Ennerdale Bridge.
Kinniside Stone Circle.

2.0km (25.2km) /   1.25mi (15.75mi)
Ennerdale Bridge
Shop, 2 PHs.

8.8km (34.0km) / 5.5mi (21.25mi)
High Gillerthwaite
Ennerdale YHA hostel and High Gillerthwaite YHA Camping
Barn. Just before this: Low Gillerthwaite Field Centre - accepts
walkers.

5.4km (39.4km) / 3.4mi (24.6mi)
Black Sail Hut
YHA hostel.

4.6km (44.0km) / 2.9mi (27.3mi)
Honister
Honister Hause YHA hostel. Slate mine has teashop.

3.0km (47.0km) / 1.9mi (29.2mi)
Seatoller

1.5km (48.5km) / 1mi (30.1mi)
Borrowdale
Borrowdale YHA hostel.

0.5km (49.0km) / 0.3mi (30.4mi)
Rosthwaite
Shop, hotel/PH, WC.

12.2km (61.2km) / 7.6mi (38.0mi)
Grasmere
Grasmere Independent Hostel, Broadrayne Farm, CA22 9RU,

Grasmere Butharlyp Howe YHA hostel, PH, outdoor shop.

1.0km (62.2km) / 0.6mi (38.6mi)
Mill Bridge
PH.

11.0km (73.2km) / 6.8mi (45.5mi)
Patterdale
Camping/bunkhouse: Heather Jackson, Noran Bank Farm, CA11 0NR - 1.5km south.   Side Farm Camping - 1km north. Patterdale YHA hostel, shops, PO, PHs, ATM.
Possible sightings of red deer, golden eagle. High Street = old Roman road. Kidsty Pike (780m / 2,560ft) is the highest point on the CTC.

24.4km (97.6km) / 15.2mi (60.6mi)
Shap
PO, PHs, ATM, WCs.
Shap Abbey.
4km / 2.5mi after Shap: Oddendale stone circle.

14.0km (111.6km) / 8.7mi (69.3mi)
Orton
Shops, PO, PHs, ATM, tearoom.
Limestone pavements before Orton.
2km / 1.25mi after Orton: Gamelands stone circle.

> 2km (113.6) / 1.25mi (70.6mi)
> (and 0.7km / 0.4mi off route)
> *Raisbeck*
> Campsite.

> 8.5km (122.1km) / 5.3mi (75.9mi)
> (and 0.3km / 0.2mi off route)
> *Bents Farm*
> Bunkhouse.

1km / 0.6mi after Bents Fm: Severals settlement on Begin Hill.
0.5km / 0.3mi on: Smardalegill Viaduct (to north).
3km / 1.9mi on: pass under Settle-Carlisle Railway.

20.1km (131.7km) / 12.5mi (81.8mi)
Kirkby Stephen
B&B, camping, shops, PO, PH, ATM, hostel.
7km / 4.3mi on: Nine Standards Rigg. Pick appropriate path from here to Keld.

18.4km (150.1km) / 11.4mi (93.3mi)
Keld
Campsite, PH, WC.
Old lead mines on way to Gunnerside.
Choose route from Keld to Reeth: 1) Over Swinner Gill and Reeth High Moor (old lead mines, industrial archaeology, etc), 2) Along River Swale (fields of wild flowers), or 3) Poor weather alternative along road.

> 1km (151.1km) / 0.6mi (93.9mi)
> (and 3km / 1.9mi off route)
> *Muker*
> B&B, hostel, campsite, café-shop.

> (3km / 1.9mi off route, 4km / 2.5mi on from Muker)
> *Gunnerside*
> B&B, PO, PH, tearooms.

> (2km / 1.25mi off route, 8km / 5mi on from Gunnerside)
> *How Hill*
> Low Row YHA Camping Barn.

17.0km (167.1km) / 10.6mi (103.8mi)
Reeth
B&B, shop, PH, WC, PO, cafes, outdoor shop.

1km (168.1km) / 0.6mi (104.5mi)
(and 1km / 0.6mi off route)
Grinton
Grinton Lodge YHA hostel.

13.0km (180.1km) / 8.1mi (111.9mi)
East Applegarth
East Applegarth Camping Barn.

4.0km (184.1km) / 2.5mi (114.4mi)
Richmond
Shops, PO, PHs, ATM, WC, B&Bs.
Richmond Castle.
Flat stretch of route to Ingleby Cross.

3.8km (187.9km) / 2.4mi (116.7mi)
Colburn Hall
Camping, PH.

3km (190.9km) / 1.9mi (118.6mi)
(and 1km / 0.6mi off route)
Brompton-on-Swale
Brompton YHA Camping Barn, PO, PHs.

3.6km (191.5km) / 2.2mi (119mi)
Catterick Bridge
Camping, PH.

1.5km (193km) / 0.9mi (119.9mi)
(and 0.5km / 0.3mi off route)
Scorton
PH, PO, WC.

13.0km (204.5km) / 8.1mi (127.1mi)
Danby Wiske
Hotel, camping, B&B, PH, café.
Lowest inland point on CTC: 35m / 115ft.

3km (207.5km) / 1.9mi (128.9mi)
(and 0.5km / 0.3mi off route)
Lovesome Hill
Bunkhouse, camping.

14.0km (218.5km) / 8.7mi (135.8mi)
Ingleby Cross
B&B, camping, PH, PO.

2.5km (221km) / 1.6mi (137.3mi)
(and 1km / 0.6mi off route)
Osmotherley
B&B, shop, PO, PH, camping, Osmotherley YHA
hostel.

6.5km (227.5km) / 4mi (141.4mi)
(and 1km / 0.6mi off route)
Swainby
PO, PHs, WC.

14.4km (232.9km) / 8.9mi (144.7mi)
Lord Stones
Café.
4km / 2.5mi on: Wain Stones.

4.0km (236.9km) / 2.5mi (147.2mi)
Clay Bank Top
3km / 1.9mi on: Face Stone on Round Hill.

14.4km (251.3km) / 8.8mi (156.1mi)
Lion Inn, Blakey
PH, camping, B&Bs in nearby villages.

14.4km (265.7km) / 8.9mi (165.1mi)
Glaisdale
B&B, camping, PH, WC, PO, shop.

11.0km (276.7km) / 6.8mi (171.9mi)
Egton Bridge
PHs, WC.

2.1km (278.8km) / 1.3mi (173.2mi)
Priory Farm
Camping.

0.8km (279.6km) / 0.5mi (173.7mi)
Grosmont
B&B, camping, shop, PO, PH, cafes.
1.5km / 0.9mi on: Low Bride Stones, High Bride Stones.

5.4km (285.0km) / 3.4mi (177.1mi)
Littlebeck
1.5km 0.9mi on: Falling Foss waterfall and Midge Hall (tea garden).

8.4km (293.4km) / 5.2mi (182.3mi)
Middle Rigg
Camping.

5.0km (298.4km) / 3.1mi (185.4mi)
Hawsker
B&B, camping with café, PH.

1.4km (299.8km) / 0.9mi (186.3mi)
Hawsker Bottoms
Camping, café.

5.8km (309km) / 3.6mi (192mi)
Robin Hood's Bay
B&Bs, hotels, camping, PHs, PO, WC, Boggle Hole YHA Hostel, Wainwright's Bar.

Chapter 10

Trip Planning

Accommodation

Pre-booking accommodation with baggage transfer can be reassuring and makes the walk very manageable: if you need something but don't have it on you, it will only be a few hours before you're reunited with your luggage and your equipment in that night's guest-house or pub. The downside of this approach, of course, is that you'll find your walking itinerary and, in particular your daily mileage, taken out of your hands and instead determined by your accommodation choices.

The definitive guide to accommodation on and around the Coast to Coast is written by Doreen Whitehead, a former bed and breakfast owner on the CtoC. Mrs Whitehead's guide is updated every year and its cost is minimal. The latest copy can easily be found by a quick web search. It pays to book well in advance, of course, especially in summer.

My preference, camping, has many advantages over pre-booked accommodation but suffers from the single disadvantage that you'll need to carry your kit. That said, and strange though it sounds, I found that as a backpacker I was often carrying less than many day-walkers were. It is possible to backpack the CtoC and to camp without carrying heaps of equipment.

There are campsites along the Coast to Coast route (see the route data in Chapter 9), but it's also possible to wild camp without problems, or to mix camping with the occasional night in a hostel, so as to dry oneself out or do laundry.

If you're considering wild camping (i.e. camping other than on a campsite) it helps to know the law on the subject.

Wild camping is not illegal in England. It's regarded as courteous to ask the landowner's permission, provided you can work out who owns the land, but that's rarely possible in the hills or up on the moor. The golden rules are: leave no trace and do no damage; minimise your impact by pitching camp late and striking camp early.

If a landowner or their agent should ask you to leave, then do so promptly and politely; if you refuse to leave when asked, they are entitled to use reasonable force to remove you. With the exception of certain specialised areas such as railways, nuclear premises and diplomatic missions, trespass is not normally a criminal matter, which means the police will not usually be interested. On the rare occasions I've had a conversation with farmers about camping on their land, I've found them to be very reasonable.

Equipment

Equipment needs will vary according to accommodation preference. Walkers going "into brick" every night, i.e. staying in pubs, bed and breakfast (B&Bs for short), hostels or hotels, will not need the same equipment as someone who camps.

The Route Assessment in Chapter 8 shows you the likely weather conditions to be expected at whatever time of year you decide to hike. Take insulation, rainwear and sun protection appropriate to those conditions. Good information increases the likelihood of taking appropriate clothing and can help keep pack weight to a minimum. Cotton is best avoided because it retains water when wet and can quickly chill the wearer; synthetic material which dries quickly is more practical.

Below are outline equipment lists for non-campers and campers: pick one, use it as a starting point and personalise it to your needs.

Kit List for Pubs, Hostels, B&Bs, etc.

Walkers staying in pubs, hostels, and/or B&B type accommodation, and having their luggage sent ahead by courier service, can be lavish with what they take. That said, choosing carefully from your suitcase each morning should ensure that you carry the absolute minimum on your back each day. As far as possible, let the courier service do the carrying! A possible kit list might look something like this:

Daysack
Shirt
Trousers (US: pants)
Underwear
Socks
Footwear
Gaiters
Fleece top (lightweight insulation)
Woolly hat
Gloves
Sun hat
Sun cream
Water bottle
Map (see section on maps below)
Map case
Compass
GPS (optional) and batteries
Headtorch
Whistle (less tiring than shouting if you need to attract the attention of rescuers)
Emergency kit (see "Contingency Planning" below)
Camera
Trekking poles
Sit mat (a warm, comfortable, dry place to sit when you take a break or eat lunch - cheap and light)
Money, documents, mobile phone, etc.
Spare clothes (in luggage, moved by courier)

Kit List for Campers

Hikers who are camping will need all of the above plus camping kit. The weight of my kit (i.e. everything except food and water) was 6.5kg (14lbs). It's possible to go even lighter than that, so it really isn't necessary to weigh yourself down. In addition to the list above, campers might wish to consider:

Rucksack/pack
Tent
Sleeping mat
Sleeping bag
Stove and fuel
Mug
Spoon
Water bladders
Water purifying tablets (water purifying tablets will usually suffice to create clean water - avoid water where sheep or cattle defecate)
Washing kit (cleansing wipes / moist towelettes, toothbrush, toothpaste, toilet paper, deodorant, liquid soap for laundry and for showers if you overnight at a hostel or campsite)
Flip flops (UK/US) to wear in showers (Aus/NZ: thongs)

If you're carrying them constantly, it pays to keep spare clothes to a minimum. My spare clothes consisted of:
One shirt
One pair underpants
One pair socks
Nothing else

Navigation

Most guidebooks contain maps of the route, but books tend to be heavy and they're not always practicable to use in bad weather. Guidebooks are very useful when you're in the planning stage of a trip, and they could go into your couriered luggage so that you can consult them each evening if you wish.

Harvey Maps produce two strip maps which cover the Coast to Coast at a scale of 1:40,000 (2.5cm to the kilometre).

Titled *The Coast to Coast West* and *The Coast to Coast East*, they are excellent maps, designed for the walker, and they show the usual route with its seasonal variations. They're printed on a tough, lightweight material which is also waterproof, so there's no need to add the weight of a map case.

There is a significant weight saving in carrying strip maps. The two Harvey's maps weigh in at 135g (4.75oz) for both of them. The nine 1:50,000 Ordnance Survey maps required to cover the route, with a waterproof map case, weigh a total of 780g (27.5oz).

The downside of strip maps is that they leave the user blind to anything off the narrow strip along which he or she is walking. If you're wondering what those hills are on the horizon, you'll still be wondering after checking the map because the chances are they won't be on it.

The Ordnance Survey produce mapping at scales of 1:25,000 and 1:50,000. As noted, you'll need a lot of them to cover the whole Coast to Coast Walk, but if you're using a baggage courier service that needn't be a problem: you can just carry the ones you use each day. Do put them in a clear, waterproof map cover though, or you risk them turning to *papier mache* in the rain. The OS produce all their maps in laminated waterproof editions but these come at an extra cost and they're heavier.

You'll need twelve of the 1:25,000 maps (sold as *OS Explorer* maps) if you choose that scale (with a map case, over a kilo in weight – about two and a quarter pounds). That said, the 1:25,000 maps are extraordinarily well detailed and they show field boundaries which can be very useful for navigation. Look for *OS Explorer* map numbers 4, 5, 6, 7, 19, 26, 27, 30, 31, 302, 303 and 304.

If you prefer the 1:50,000 scale, and it's a perfectly acceptable scale for this walk, you'll need nine *OS Landranger* maps: numbers 89, 90, 91, 92, 93, 94, 98, 99, and 100.

If you choose the Ordnance Survey maps, of whatever scale, be sure to mark your intended route on them before you set out – the Coast to Coast route isn't printed on OS maps because it isn't a national trail, in accordance with Wainwright's wishes that walkers devise their own route.

The Coast to Coast Walk is not waymarked throughout its entire length, although there is the occasional signpost here and there. For that reason, it would be very unwise to rely solely on signs.

The route crosses moors and mountains which are subject to frequent bad weather at any time of the year. This can reduce visibility quickly and substantially.

As a minimum, walkers should be able to read a map and to use it with a compass. GPS can be useful as an adjunct to a map and compass, but it's not a complete replacement.

Fitness

The Coast to Coast Walk doesn't require an unusually high level of fitness, but it is more enjoyable if you are fit enough to walk it before you start.

Gather together all the equipment you intend to carry each day and put it into your pack. Will you be able to carry it for 15-20 miles a day, day after day, up hill and down dale, in the clothes and shoes you plan to wear?

If not, it's possible you'll need to lighten your load and it's probable you'll need to do some pre-hike training. Don't rely on getting "hill fit" on the hill. Any physical training which increases your strength, stamina and endurance in advance of your hike will be helpful, and the closer it approximates to walking long distances with your pack on, the better.

Getting There and Getting Back

The Coast to Coast is not a circular walk, so you'll finish many miles away from where you started.

Both ends of the walk are accessible by public transport.

St Bees isn't on any scheduled coach routes but it does have a railway station. Check with National Rail and remember that English train companies offer substantial discounts if you book well in advance.

The railway station at Robin Hood's Bay closed in 1965,

but there is an excellent bus service to nearby Scarborough, which is well-connected by rail and only three hours from London.

Food and Water

If you're staying in pre-booked accommodation each night then food planning is unlikely to be of much interest to you. With breakfast and an evening meal securely booked, and with lunch provided by last night's host, you'll only have to think about anything you need to top up what you're given, or any special dietary requirements. Should you need to supplement your food supply, you'll pass enough shops, pubs and tea rooms to do so without too much difficulty (see the route data Chapter 9 for details).

If you need to refill your water bottle, most mountain streams are safe to drink from, especially if you treat the water with purifying tablets (readily available online at a minimal cost). Avoid the water from lowland streams, particularly in areas grazed by cattle (which includes most of the Vale of Mowbray).

If you're camping, no-one's going to slap a meal in front of you at regular intervals and so food planning becomes much more important. You'll be able to get meals at various points along your hike (again, check the route data), so you only need to plan food to fill the gaps where you won't be able to get meals, with maybe a little in hand for unforeseen events.

Once you've worked out how much food you'll need, consider how much of it you want to carry at any given time. I'd suggest three days' worth is a reasonable maximum if you want to walk in relative comfort. The remainder can be parcelled up and posted ahead to post offices, hostels, etc., and then collected as you pass. Check the post office website for details of branches and their current opening times. To send a food parcel *post restante*, address it to:

Your name
Post restante
Full address of the Post Office branch, with postcode.

118

Don't forget to take a photographic form identification, such as your passport, when you collect it.

There is also plenty of scope to re-supply in village shops as you pass them.

Blisters

Blisters can ruin your hike, but they are avoidable.

The main causes of blisters, either singly or in combination, are:

1. Friction, for example from footwear which is too tight or too loose, or from trail debris getting into the shoe;

2. Moisture, such as sweat, or water from bogs, streams or puddles, which softens and puckers the skin and makes it prone to blistering; and/or,

3. Heat, which causes the foot to sweat, swell and rub against the inside of the shoe.

It follows then, that the more effectively these three variables are controlled, the less the chance of blisters

Friction can be reduced by selecting well-fitting footwear, by wearing long trousers or gaiters to keep trail debris out of the shoe, by taping the foot with athletic tape, by applying lubricant to the foot, and by applying colloidal "gel" plasters to "hotspots" before they develop into blisters.

Moisture can be managed by a well-considered choice of socks and shoes, and by the application of foot balm or foot powder.

Heat can be regulated by choosing shoes and socks of a type appropriate to your route assessment.

Very few blisters emerge without the hiker becoming aware of them at an early stage. Don't try to "tough it out": if you feel a hot spot developing, stop and deal with it. Think through the main causes: friction, moisture and/or heat: which ones apply and how can you manage them to reduce their effects? Apply tape and gel plasters at the first twinge - you can always discard them later if it proves to be a false alarm.

Contingencies

Contingency planning means doing your emergency thinking well in advance, and thus under no pressure, rather than in the heat of an emergency, possibly miles from anywhere and in bad weather. Some potential problems are:

Serious Injury/Illness

A serious injury or illness is one which is going to end my hike. If I can keep on walking, I can reach help. If I can't continue walking, I have a bigger problem because I have to get help to me. Survival experts talk about the "Rule of Threes", which tells us that humans can survive:

Three hours without shelter in extreme conditions;

Three days without water; and,

Three weeks without food.

If an illness or an injury prevents me from walking, I have the shelter issue covered because I have a tent in my pack. Walkers not carrying a tent (for instance, those staying in pubs, hostels, bed and breakfast, etc.) might find it worth carrying a lightweight bivvy bag or a survival sack for this eventuality.

I'll usually have some water with me, and water tends to be close by in British hills (sometimes too close!). I'll also have some food, although food isn't quite so much of an issue.

My route assessment tells me that I can't rely on my mobile phone in an emergency because I won't have a signal on most of the route, and particularly in the most remote parts of it. But I'm walking one of the most famous walks in the world, one trodden by thousands of people each year, through areas which also attract lots of day walkers. Provided I haven't strayed too far from the Coast to Coast route or one of its seasonal variants, someone is going to pass me before very long.

I carry a small whistle to attract an attention in an emergency, because it's light in weight and blowing it is less tiring than shouting.

Minor Injury/Illness

I carry a lightweight emergency kit (details below) which,

amongst other things, contains items for the treatment of minor ailments including blisters, insect bites, diarrhoea and minor pain.

Equipment Failure

Working on the basis that "if it can't be repaired with duct tape, you're not using enough duct tape", I usually carry a few metres of the stuff wrapped around an old credit card. It weighs very little, yet gives me some capacity to make repairs to my tent, shoes, coat, etc., should I need to. I also carry some twine which doubles as a clothes line when I wash my few items of clothing.

Personal Safety

Despite what some newspapers would have us believe, crime in England is relatively low. The Coast to Coast Walk passes through some very calm, very crime-free rural areas. Hiking alone is not a difficult proposition and it can be done quite safely, indeed, Wainwright often hiked alone.

It's always good practice to leave an itinerary with a friend or a relative (a copy of your data sheet would do just as well) but bear in mind that, even though the UK is densely populated, you will be walking through isolated countryside for most of the hike: expect mobile phone coverage to be intermittent at best.

Wet Kit

I know that if my kit gets wet, apart from a fortuitous spell of good weather, I have no options to dry it on the trail. I can only wait for better weather or get to a hostel or a pub. That fact makes me very careful to isolate my down sleeping bag, my camera and my spare clothes in a waterproof bag to keep them dry. Most other items will still function if they get wet.

Emergency Kit

I carry a small emergency kit which varies slightly from trip to trip, according to my route assessment. This is what it contained for the Coast to Coast Walk:

Colloidal gel blister plasters in assorted sizes
Moleskin
Athletic tape
Ibuprofen tablets
Paracetamol tablets
Anti-histamine tablets
Anti-diarrhoea tablets
Antiseptic cream
Tick remover
Lighter
Spare water purifying tablets
Duct tape
Spare head torch batteries
Twine

Useful Websites

Accommodation
Doreen Whitehead's accommodation guide:
www.coasttocoastguides.co.uk/accommodation.htm

Post Offices
Post Office branch finder (addresses and opening times):
www.postoffice.co.uk/branch-finder

Trail Information
The Wainwright Society:
www.wainwright.org.uk/coasttocoast.html

Travel
National Rail journey planner:
http://ojp.nationalrail.co.uk/service/planjourney/search

Arriva bus journey planner (Robin Hood's Bay to Scarborough, to connect with the national rail system at

Scarborough):

http://app.arrivabus.co.uk/journeyplanner/query/en?

Glossary of Terms

Beck: a stream.

Crag: a rough, steep rock face.

Dale: a valley (also part of place names, e.g. Borrowdale, Easedale).

Edge: a cliff or escarpment.

Fell: a hill or mountain.

Force: a waterfall.

Gill / ghyll: a small, steep-sided valley.

How: a low hill.

Knott: a craggy hill.

Mere: a lake. (Also included in place names, making the word "lake" redundant. "Lake Windermere" for instance, should read simply "Windermere". The "mere" already signifies that it's a lake.)

Pike: a sharp, pointed hill.

Rake: a path up a hill or gully.

Tarn: a small lake.

Thwaite: land reclaimed from forest or wetlands, often included in place names (Rosthwaite, Seathwaite).

Index

A

B

C

About the Author

John Davison started hiking and camping on school trips and in the Scouts, during the early 1970s. Exploring new places, meeting new people and discovering how the two interrelate is an interest which has never left him.

John is a Fellow of the Royal Geographical Society and he lives in Essex, UK.

Other books by John Davison

Every Day Above a New Horizon

In 1878 Robert Louis Stevenson, the author of *Treasure Island* and *Kidnapped*, walked across the south of France with a donkey. His plan was to write an account of his journey and to use the proceeds to fund a trip across the Atlantic to re-join the love of his life in the USA.

Inspired by Stevenson's account, John Davison finds himself constrained by his job in London and by his family commitments. Far from making things better, a series of short hiking trips in the UK only serve to fan the flame until, finally, the opportunity presents itself.

John sets off in Stevenson's footsteps, sensibly without the donkey, through blazing sun and driving rain, across one of the least populated parts of Europe; encountering kind, generous people, leavened with the occasional idiot, meeting them all with an keen eye and a dry sense of humour as he heads towards journey's end: the golden city down on the plain.

This is the art of the possible: John tells the story of one man's journey with just enough "how-to" to inspire you to start your own...

If you are old enough, you'll remember the Apollo space missions taking off from Cape Kennedy. And you might remember the countdown, 10, 9, 8 and so on, right down to zero! At that point, right when you might have expected the rocket to soar up into the sky, nothing happened. Well, nothing obvious happened. In reality, of course, there was lots going on. All systems were go, the engines had fired and were now building up power to thrust the huge rocket into space. At zero! there wasn't much to see, but we all knew that something momentous was about to happen.

So it was in the back bar of the Ardlui Hotel. There wasn't anything obvious to see, but everyone knew that something was going to happen...

Reviewers say:

"A truly inspiring read, written from the heart of a man with enthusiasm and passion for walking."

"A great story teller."

"Highly recommended not only as a traveller's tale but also a guide to wild camping."

"A great book to have in your bag."

A Spring Ramble – Walking the Offa's Dyke Path

Offa's Dyke.

The border between England and Wales.

1,200 years old and 177 miles long.

More ascent than Everest.

The most impressive monument of its kind in Europe, now a national walking trail.

The present-day peace and tranquillity of this beautiful, remote area belie its turbulent past. Follow the walk from sea to sea, past castles, battlegrounds and ancient churches, over mountains and alongside rivers. Discover the history of this fascinating, enchanting region and some of the personalities who ruled, fought, built, farmed, robbed, wrote, painted and campaigned here.

Connect with Me

For help planning your own trip, check my website at

      www.johndavison.moonfruit.com

If you have any questions, email me via the "Contact" button and I'll do my best to answer them.

Keep up-to-date with my latest adventure by following me on Twitter: @bootsonthehill.

Happy trekking!